FranklinCovey Co.
2200 West Parkway Blvd.
Salt Lake City, UT 84119

Printed in the United States of America

First edition printing June 2014

ISBN 978-1-936111-59-6

www.franklincovey.com

Special Thanks To:
Carly Frazier - Cover and Book design
Alicia Bonilla - Editing

MILLENNIALS
@WORK

The 7 Skills Every TWENTY-SOMETHING
(And Their Manager) Needs to
OVERCOME ROADBLOCKS and ACHIEVE GREATNESS

Contents

THIS IS NOT AN INTRODUCTION *(So please don't skip it.)*

It's about time someone reached out a hand and explained just what is going on at work. This book is a collection of findings and insights that will help you rock the workplace. After all, it's your destiny. Enjoy!

A PROMISE TO YOU

If you read this book, you will have a successful career and live happily ever after. You'll probably be named CEO by Friday. We're already looking forward to your nomination as Time Magazine's Person of the Year.

Actually, you are probably already well on your way to your happily ever after and that is why you are intrigued by this book. You have high expectations of yourself and represent high hopes for the people in your life who have enthusiastically invested in you. Up until now, your environment has been designed to be supportive of your dreams and pursuits. School, sports, activities, and home have been filled with fans you know to be "for you." But here comes the part in the movie where the unsuspecting character enters a dark, foreboding alley. The music changes and you know something dramatic, potentially even awful, is about to happen. In this book, the unsuspecting character is you. And the dark alley? It's work.

Work life is different from anything you have experienced up to this point. Not because it is work, but because authority figures at work may appear very different from those you have encountered in your life so far. It is not an overstatement to say that many young professionals

Using years of research to back our advice, we've written what we hope is a helpful tool, one that will help you identify potential roadblocks in your career so you'll know exactly what to do when you encounter them.

experience a hefty dose of culture shock when they enter the workforce. The promise of this book is to help you understand the challenges that can stand in the way of success and teach you the skills necessary for achieving greatness at work. Going back to our movie analogy, this book is our way of shouting, "Look out! Don't go that way!" Using years of research to back our advice, we've written what we hope is a helpful tool, one that will help you identify potential roadblocks in your career so you'll know exactly what to do when you encounter them. On the other hand, we are aware that there are some challenges you can't do a thing about, like an unusually high unemployment rate for people under 30, or the ever-rising interest rates on your school loans. But when it comes to achieving success at work — or avoiding that dark alley altogether — there is a lot you can do.

A PROMISE TO YOUR PARENTS

If your son or daughter reads this book, all their problems will be solved and they'll live happily ever after. At the very least, they'll be awesome at work and won't have to live in your basement.

Many parents understand the frustration of sacrificing time and resources for their young adult's future, only to see their child struggle and stumble as they transition into work life. Sometimes the frustration is with your son or daughter rather than with their experiences, but more often than not, your aggravation is the result of an organization not seeing the same greatness in your child that you do. In this book, we'll offer counsel to your young professional on how their generation (Millennials or Gen Y) is perceived in the workplace, why it matters, and what they can do to succeed in spite of challenging generational differences.

A PROMISE TO YOUR MANAGER

If your Millennial employee reads this book, they'll rock the office and your expectations. Not only that, they'll actually make you a better human being. Think of all the stress and money you'll save when you're no longer in therapy for trying to understand them! Oh, and your hair will look great, too (a result of no longer pulling it out every day).

With the exception of Pointy-Haired Boss , most managers want to be succesful at what they do. When it comes to managing Millennials, managers *really* want to do well. But there's an obvious disconnect between the generations that can make the successful managing of them a little more difficult than milking a unicorn. The benefit of this book is that as Millennial employees read about and implement the skills discussed here, they'll come to you armed with everything you wish they already knew. Perhaps you can celebrate your mutual future success over a fresh glass of unicorn milk!

ROADBLOCKS

We've made it a third of the way through this Non-Introduction and have earned a break. Let's take a brief mental vacation, shall we? Imagine yourself on a road trip. You're on your way to somewhere amazing, you're enjoying the beautiful scenery around you. All is well as you turn up the music and accelerate. Aaaaaah ... the wind in your hair, the sun on your face, a full tank

An American comic strip created by Scott Adams, Dilbert is well-known for its satirical look at typical, white-collar, micromanaged offices in Anytown, USA. The humor must be universally understood, however — the cartoon is printed in 2,000 newspapers worldwide, in 65 countries and 25 languages. Pointy-Haired Boss is known for making life at work for Dilbert nothing short of miserable.

of gas. And just like that, out of nowhere, BAM! (Mental break ends here.) A roadblock?! In the middle of your trip? How can this be? How long will it take to get around it? Where do you go from here? This isn't fair! This wasn't the plan!!

Your work life is a similar journey that will have unexpected twists, turns, ups, downs, even a few delays, but we're here to help you get the best start — and happiest trip — possible. As you read on, watch for these sneaky roadblocks. We'll help you navigate around them by providing you with a super map for total success. Take that, Rand McNally.

RESEARCH

This book is unique because it relies on two bodies of in-depth research. The first study focused on management's perceptions of your generation in the workplace. These findings were published in *Managing the Millennials: Discover the Core Competencies for Managing Today's Workforce*. We were overwhelmed with how strongly managers reacted to our research. There was an almost universal "nod" from managers across the board, exclaiming "Yes! I'm having this problem at work!" Consequently, many leaders welcomed *Managing the Millennials* as a real-world solution for recruiting, retaining, and developing younger employees. We have since trained thousands of managers from Fortune 100 companies and up from around the world. But, you may be thinking, how does any of this help you? We'll explain.

Are you familiar with Spock from Star Trek? He used a technique called the Vulcan Mind Meld ; a telepathic link between two individuals. This link allowed a free exchange of thoughts and ideas, causing two individuals to become, essentially, one mind. Whenever Mr. Spock needed information, he simply mind-melded. In essence, we want to help you mind-meld.

 To enhance the Vulcan Mind Meld, try adding sound effects. Fill Slurpee cup with Slurpee of choice. Place Slurpee straw flush against bottom of cup. Suck Slurpee loudly while reading about Spock's technique. Slurpee-straw-sucking should sound pretty much like mind-melding.

We don't recommend you try this trick on your next date, but rather with your managers and leaders so you can better understand how they see your generation in the workplace. We'll let you in on the perceptions managers have of younger workers; perceptions we learned about as we conducted research for this book. And while we know it's unfair to say that all Millennial employees are the same, unfortunately your manager's perceptions don't have to be — and most often are not — based in reality. Perceptions often lead to managerial behaviors, which then trickle down as roadblocks. Unfortunately, the very same roadblocks that can stand in your way of success.

The second study, "Millennial Integration: Challenges Millennials Face in the Workplace and What They Can Do About Them" focused on challenges (a.k.a. roadblocks) younger workers reported having as they entered the workforce. Our data comes from young professionals from all over the world. We asked, "What is the biggest challenge you face in the workplace?" In the following chapters, you will get insight from your Millennial peers on what to expect at work and how you can overcome the things that block your path. If you have been in the workforce for a while, you'll be able to relate to the

challenges these participants talk about and find the seven skills we suggest to be practical, relevant, and effective.

While conducting studies to identify the specific challenges Millennials were facing at work, there was a concern that our sample lacked a wider representation of industries and organizations. Obviously, workplace culture would differ between organizations (at times, dramatically), and by representing a limited sampling of companies and employees, we would in turn limit the global bearing of our findings. To address this concern, additional Millennials were invited to participate in a web-based survey. We invited hundreds of Millennial professionals to answer the same questions we had asked previous participants.

We noticed that the additional group of respondents had an average tenure of 5.5 years in the workforce. After analyzing the data from the more experienced group, no marked difference in responses between first- and second-wave Millennials were found (we define first-wave Millennials as entering the workforce before 2010). Because these respondents had been in the workforce for a significant period of time, we asked what they had done to overcome the work-related challenges they had identified.

This produced some unique insight, resulting in a collection of exciting findings which clearly identified the most common — and seemingly universal — roadblocks Millennials face in the workplace today.

This produced some unique insight, resulting in a collection of exciting findings which clearly identified the most common — and seemingly universal — roadblocks Millennials face in the workplace today. One more thing about this second round of findings: the observation that first- and second-wave Millennials reported the same challenges, even though their time in the workforce differed by years, suggests that managers and organizations have indeed been slow to adapt to the new employees coming on the scene. This should prove all the more motivation to put the skills to work!

CAPE AND TIGHTS OPTIONAL

Our goal really is focused on helping managers and younger workers work together successfully. As we've trained managers and Millennials, we find that both are eager to start a discussion about the other one's need to adapt and do things differently. Our response to managers is that the people with the most responsibility have to adapt first. While Millennials definitely need to make adjustments as they integrate into the workforce, it is our belief that if people in management positions want to experience any degree of success, they'll have to change and adapt as well.

Interestingly, the perceptions of managers and the roadblocks of younger workers aligned almost perfectly. Thrilling from a researcher's perspective, but not so thrilling from yours. As a Millennial, you're basically getting served a double-whammy sunny-side up, minus the side of buttery, crunchy toast. Perceptions and roadblocks have joined forces, so you need to be armed with skills to overcome. With your cape securely fastened and your tights sufficiently snugged, no way will these roadblocks stop you from getting what you expect and want from your work life!

Lastly, it is not our intent to merely point out the roadblocks. Our objective is to help you overcome them by explaining why it is important for you to adapt, where you can adapt, and how you can adapt. In each of the seven skill chapters (Chapters 4 - 10), we will present a research-proven roadblock, its associated managerial perception, and a handy skill to help you tackle every obstacle. When put into practice, these skills will equip you to take control of your career — with or without cape and tights.

Chapter 1

WHAT'S A MILLENNIAL AND WHERE DO I FIT IN?

If an online gaming habit has convinced you that world domination is the way to go, this little fact will make your day: by the year 2025, your generation will dominate the workforce, and we don't mean by a little bit. MILLENNIALS. WILL. DOMINATE. THE. WORLD. At work, in politics, and in business, your generation will become the world's future leaders. But only those who are fast enough and good enough at adapting in the workplace will be among them. Will you?

YOU ARE HERE
(YOUR PLACE IN HISTORY)

Welcome to the game of business and work, Millennials! As a generation, you are more diverse and educated than any generation before you. You are also the first generation (thanks to the web) that doesn't need an authority figure to gain access to information, resulting in a unique and advanced group of workers. You are the world's first global generation as well, connected by the Internet, email, social media, and your sheer desire to — what else? — connect! In fact, a whopping 75 percent of you have an online presence through at least one social networking site, compared to 50 percent of Gen Xers and only 30 percent of Boomers[1].

Demographically, in 2009 the Millennial generation was predominantly white at 61 percent of the population, followed by 19 percent Hispanic, 14 percent black, five percent Asian, and the remaining percentage falling in the 'other' category[2]. Your peers are more ethnically and racially diverse than older adults, including the Gen Xers just one generation before you. Statistically, Millennials are less religious (but that doesn't mean less spiritual), less likely to serve in the military, and on track to becoming the best educated.

Unlike the generations that have preceded you in punching the proverbial time clock Monday through Friday, your generation is going to work, learning to work, and working in a completely different way than at any other time in history. The things that motivate your generation to work have changed, and what you hope to gain from work is different than what your parents and grandparents wanted.

Millennials are also entering the workforce later in life than previous generations. It isn't uncommon to hear your grandparents talk about their first job at the local grocery store, punching the clock as a 13- or 14-year-old. The Boomers and Xers also started working in their teens, while most Millennials and NextGens won't start their first job until their late teens or upon entering college. Since the Bureau of Labor Statistics first began recording workplace data in 1948, the 47 percent of 16-to-24-year-olds who are employed today is the smallest share of a generation's workers in the Bureau's statistical history[3]. In 2011, 37 percent of people aged 18-29 were unemployed[4]. Unemployment among your peers is over 40 percent, at least three times as high as in any previous generation's work history. Though the recession and economic crisis of the 21st century have undoubtedly played a role in these numbers, Millennials are also hesitant to settle (and settle down!) for less than what they expect. This gap in working age is partly responsible for what you want from your job and life. You expect more, at times you even demand more. And chances are, your boss isn't going to be used to that.

In the past, generations worked mainly to secure comfort and livelihood: a white-picket fence, the American dream, or building a sizable nest egg with the goal of making life better for posterity. The focus was mainly on family and providing a comfortable life for them. On the flip side, Millennials have been much slower to get married and begin families. With 75 percent of your generation still single, demographers and scholars have noted that perhaps other goals and priorities have outshined the focus of older generations on the family and home.

Recognizing that your life and experiences are rarely 'one size fits all,' for the most part, your generation has had it bit easier. Your generation isn't driven to secure the basic necessities of life, but by a deeper need to do something, be something, create something, and to reap the satisfaction and reward of making a difference in the world. Your focus has been allowed to shift more onto you, and you've been raised this way from birth by the adults that surround you. In our work with Millennials, we've seen some common trends in just what it is you expect from work as well as the opinions you share about it. Check out these numbers:

MILLENNIALS@WORK

 7 out of 10 Millennials think they need "me time" at work.

3 out of 5 Millennials feel that they will switch jobs in less than five years.

1 out of 4 Millennials say they are completely satisfied with their current job.

4 out of 5 Millennials think they deserve to be recognized more for their work.

 9 out of 10 Millennials think they deserve their dream job.

THE MILLENNIAL TAKEOVER

Even with Baby Boomers delaying retirement, the U.S. Bureau of Labor Statistics predicts Millennials will make up more than half of the workforce by 2015 and over 75% by the year 2030. PwC, a global accounting firm, did an internal employee audit and project that by 2016 almost 80 percent of their workforce will be comprised of Millennials.[4] By sheer number, you will have an undeniable impact on the business world. According to the U.S. Census Bureau, worldwide and within the United States, Millennials are the largest generation yet, some 2.3 billion strong.

This takeover isn't without a price, however. Millennials are more likely to job-hop than previous generations. Some estimates show turnover rates for Millennials are nearly two times higher than those of older workers. What does this mean in terms of dollars and cents? For an organization with 1,000 employees, the average annual cost of replacing Millennials — in addition to the regular expense of doing business — is a staggering $300,000. These costs can add up quickly, growing to millions of dollars a year for larger companies. Unless organizations learn to work with Millennials to improve their retention of you, that cost will only continue to skyrocket. Hypothetically, for that same 1,000-employee company, the cost of replacing Millennials due to high turnover rates would look like this:

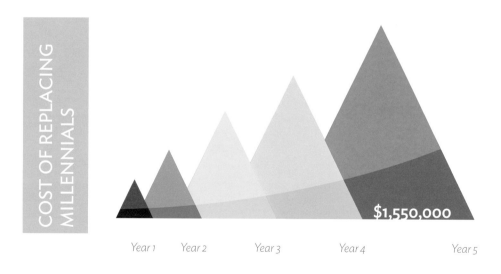

COST OF REPLACING MILLENNIALS

$1,550,000

Year 1   Year 2   Year 3   Year 4   Year 5

THE WORLD'S FIRST GLOBAL GENERATION

You have been referred to as "today's most important demographic group: the tens of millions of digital elite who are in the vanguard of a fast-emerging global youth culture."[5] Why do you think your generation is today's most important group? Demographers and researchers aren't the only ones paying attention to you. Marketers around the world are changing the way they work to cater to your generation with hopes of cashing in — big time. They understand that Millennials are more alike around the world than any other generation. When it comes to advertising, this realization comes with some significant perks! (Cha-ching!) ❓

In a *Businessweek* article "Children of the Web," writer Steve Hamm said this about Millennial digital-natives:

> *Because of smartphones, blogs, instant messaging, Flickr, MySpace, Skype, YouTube, digg, and de.lic.ious, young people scattered all over are instantly aware of what's happening to others like them everywhere else. This highly influential group, many of whom are also well-heeled, is sharing ideas and information across borders and driving demand for consumer electronics, entertainment, autos, food, and fashion. Think of it as a virtual melting pot. As the population of the young and Web-savvy grows into the hundreds of millions, the pot is going to boil.*

Marketers know that your growing number equals growing revenue. But they have to adapt their once American-centric (and somewhat technologically deficient) approach to advertising to now include the global Millennial market.

An example of this comes from a company in Japan that was quick to adapt. Tohato, a Japanese manufacturer of salty snack foods (let's just call it what it is junk food), created a way to introduce new products to young consumers while simultaneously providing free gaming. They launched a game online called "The World's Worst War" to promote two new flavors in their crunchy lineup. The interactive game allows consumers to purchase their flavor of choice, "Tyrant Habanero Burning Hot Hell" or "Satan Jorquia Bazooka Deadly Hot," and by scanning the barcode on the bag with a smart phone, enlist themselves with the corresponding army to fight in a war between the flavors. Because of Tohato's adaptive marketing to younger generations, game players and snack consumers become one and the same — conveniently, two markets that go hand in hand. How clever is that?

Who else knows that the Millennial generation holds the secret to a company's relevance and future success? Employers do. Companies are turning to the global youth demographic to recruit new talent, and they're using social networks to find the specialized skills they need.

Hamm writes about one such example of this:

> *Ning, a Silicon Valley startup with 10 nationalities represented among its 27 employees, follows blog postings and other cybertrails to find the most qualified candidates. The company provides software tools for consumers to build their own social networking sites, and it was through its own software that Ning located Fabricio Zuardi, living in remote São Carlos, Brazil.*
>
> *Unaware that his work was being noticed by Ning's recruiters, Zuardi had used Ning's company's software to build a social networking site to unite people with an interest in music. Ning engineers liked what [Zuardi] was doing and engaged him in online conversation. One day, Zuardi had the very pleasant surprise of finding a job offer from co-founder Marc Andreessen in his e-mail inbox.*

Never before in the history of the world would this kind of recruiting have been possible. Just let that sink in for a minute. Never. Before. So, why is your generation's position in the workplace so different and unique? Because you're alive at a time when previous limits, obstacles, and reluctance to worldwide interaction and growth have been eliminated by technology. Amazing. "For anyone in the world, the American dream is more accessible now," says Fabricio Zuardi. More accessible indeed, our happily-employed friend.

WHY THERE'S NO ONE ELSE LIKE YOU ON THE PLANET TODAY (EXCEPT FOR ALL THE OTHER MILLENNIALS ON THE PLANET TODAY)

Reason 1: You're Unique Because ... Your Parents Played With You

In our first book, *Managing the Millennials,* we directed our research and advice to managers belonging to older generations. Previous generations grew up in a different world, with different attitudes toward authority, so when the Millennials came into the work-picture there were some obvious conflicts. The ability of older generations to relate to and work with your generation, and vice versa, comes with effort and practice, and usually not without a few bumps in the road. In our chapter "First Them, Then You," we talked about how they could learn to engage with you in the workplace. Part of being able to do that is understanding how growing up in your world was different from growing up in theirs. (More on the art of perception-shifting later.)

In this chapter to managers, we wrote:

The ability of older generations to relate to and work with your generation, and vice versa, comes with effort and practice, and usually not without a few bumps in the road.

When they enter work life, they anticipate the same consideration they have enjoyed at home, in school, and on the playing field. They want managers who will tend to their career development and act as an advocate for them.

Millennials are used to getting a lot of positive attention and they like it. Not only do they like the attention, they expect it. When they enter work life, they anticipate the same consideration they have enjoyed at home, in school, and on the playing field. They want managers who will tend to their career development and act as an advocate for them.

One explanation for Millennial preoccupation with positive attention is the result of a subtle shift in parenting style. We believe there has been a swing from training to nurturing. That is not to say their parents (mostly Baby Boomers) did not emphasize training — they just placed a greater emphasis on nurturing.

Around the time most of your parents were busy raising your older siblings, a revolutionary voice on child rearing, Dr. Benjamin Spock, broke away from the norm and suggested a completely different approach to parenting. It was his belief that, contrary to popular opinion at the time, babies should be held and not left "to cry it out." Previously, conventional wisdom had dictated that child-rearing should focus more on building discipline, not on showing affection. He believed that showing affection toward babies did not result in spoiled children, as many thought, but rather in happier and more secure offspring. Dr. Spock was also the first pediatrician to study psychoanalysis to understand the needs of children. His ideas about childcare were so influential that subsequent generations began turning to a more flexible and affectionate approach to parenting[6].

Dr. Spock urged parents to see their children as individual and unique human beings, and to avoid a one-size-fits-all approach to parenting. But the groundbreaking idea Dr. Spock brought to the game was this: parenting could, and should, be fun. He proposed that parents could actually enjoy their children! And for the most part, your parents did just that. They enjoyed you. They encouraged you. They spent hours involved in your activities and interests, cheering you on, driving you to practice, and celebrating your victories.

We advise managers to consider this drastic difference in how younger workers were raised. All this background on child-rearing may seem irrelevant, but we assure you that it's not. The purpose of this micro-lesson on child development and parenting is this — to have a positive relationship in the workplace, older managers need to be aware of how Millennials have experienced primary authority figures in their lives and how this upbringing has influenced the Millennial value of seeking positive attention and affirmation. Likewise, Millennials need to be aware of how older generations have experienced authority in their lives. (Coming soon to a chapter near you: the ninja skill of walking in someone else's shoes.)

Reason 2: You're Unique Because ... You Is Smart

Millennials are going to college in record numbers. A larger number of graduating students are seeking postgraduate degrees. Many of your peers view education as a means to contribute to the world, and not just as a way of earning a larger paycheck. It's not just that education has become more accessible, though it has. Education today is "newer" than it was even a couple of decades ago. Advances, discoveries, and breakthroughs are happening all the time, and you want to be a part of it.

 The 2011 film "The Help," based on the novel by Kathryn Stockett set in 1960s Mississippi, portrays a maid whose love for the children in her care is expressed by the frequent affirmation, "You is kind. You is smart. You is important."

Thanks to technology and the Internet, you've learned to distance yourself from authority figures when it comes to finding information, making decisions, and forming your own opinions.

Unlike your older siblings and parents, and us and our parents, you learned leadership skills, peer counseling, problem solving, and autonomy at a very young age. Where students in previous generations enrolled in Home Ec and Shop class, you've had the option of Life Skills and leadership retreats. Thanks to technology and the Internet, you've developed a different relationship with authority figures when it comes to finding information, making decisions, and forming your own opinions. What's the result of these educational advancements and formative opportunities being handed out during your lifetime? Millions of Millennial smarties, preparing to rule the world, but lacking some of the vital skills to do it. (Never fear! This is where we come in. Vital skills to the rescue, keep reading!)

Reason 3: You're Unique Because ... You Speak.com the #Language of iTechnology

If there had to be one (and only one) factor separating you from the immense herd of humans alive and working on the planet today, it's your monumental technology skills. You boggle our minds with your whiz-bang-beeping-ringing-buzzing. And truthfully, you're a little proud of that. Millennials believe that they are superior when it comes to understanding and using technology. And, well, you are. There, we've said it. Our sometimes slow approach to understanding how to update Instagram (as in, slow like a dinosaur) is left sputtering for air as the dust of your social media skills flies by at mach speed. Cough ... gasp ... please pass our oxygen tanks.

It is this innate ability to work with and understand technology that ultimately sets you apart in the workforce. At least, our research among your peers tells us you believe this is the case. This is why some researchers refer to you and younger generations as digital-natives, literally native to the language and function of technology. The rest of us are still learning to speak and understand the language you grew up with! "Sprechen sie computer?!?"

Such advances in technology were not a part of our experience or vocabulary. In fact, a woman belonging to Generation X recently told us about her high school curriculum, where keyboarding was a required course. What's that? You haven't heard of keyboarding? It's a typing class. With a typewriter. Not an electric one. Can you believe that was only a few years prior to your stint in high school?

Reason 4: You're Unique Because … Like the Song, You've Got the Whole World In Your Hands

Millennials understand connectedness (and we don't mean the connectedness of you to your iPhone). This is a much grander belief that maybe the world isn't so big after all. You've probably seen (or might even have on your car) bumper stickers proclaiming 'One Love,' 'Envision World Peace,' or the Zen-like invitation to 'CoExist.' These mentalities and ideas belong to your generation! What used to be isolationism in other generations, has become globalization for Millennials.

Years before you were born, some of the social and cultural barriers existing in the world were as closed as the physical borders separating countries and people. International trade was limited, and countries and cultures were more unsure of one another. Information about foreign lands and foreign people was sparse, biased at times by fear or political misunderstanding. Perspectives seldom reached

First published in 1927, the children's classic spiritual "He's Got the Whole World in His Hands" should be immediately recognizable to anyone who attended Bible School or grew up with a guitar-playing youth pastor nearby. If you don't fit either of these descriptions, use the QR code below. You'll see what we mean.

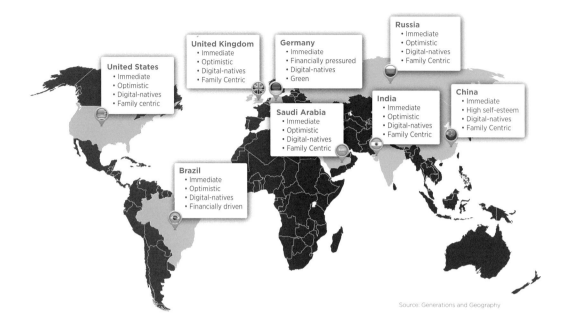

United States
- Immediate
- Optimistic
- Digital-natives
- Family centric

United Kingdom
- Immediate
- Optimistic
- Digital-natives
- Family Centric

Germany
- Immediate
- Financially pressured
- Digital-natives
- Green

Russia
- Immediate
- Optimistic
- Digital-natives
- Family Centric

Saudi Arabia
- Immediate
- Optimistic
- Digital-natives
- Family Centric

India
- Immediate
- Optimistic
- Digital-natives
- Family Centric

China
- Immediate
- High self-esteem
- Digital-natives
- Family Centric

Brazil
- Immediate
- Optimistic
- Digital-natives
- Financially driven

Source: Generations and Geography

outside the good ol' U.S.A. Rather than brainstorming ways to bring clean water to African villages or building schools for orphans in Guatemala, young people back then grew up with meat'n'taters, apple pie, baseball, and The Andy Griffith Show. And consumerism? With the exception of The Beatles, if it wasn't made, located, sung, written, built, or available for sale in the United States, it was practically obsolete.

You can probably list a hundred ways that your personal world view is different from generations before you. In fact, if you ever find yourself with an hour of free time, this could make an interesting practice. Ask your parents and older relatives to participate, too. These contrasts have led to a completely different canvas for today's business to take place on.

Here's one example of the Millennial globalization of business. Have you heard of Krochet Kids International? They got their name from a local newspaper that ran the story of three high school boys who had learned to crochet. The trio, Kohl, Travis, and Stewart, started out making snowboarding hats for themselves, but business picked up rapidly when friends began asking for custom hat orders. They eventually graduated from high school and went separate ways for college, but that was hardly the end. Kohl writes:

"During our summer breaks we volunteered in various developing nations, hoping to gain a better understanding of the global community in which we lived. It wasn't long before we came to realize how blessed we had been growing up. The desire was planted within us to help. To reach out in love. To make a difference.

It was around this time that an idea was born. One which involved a familiar trade. Friends and family encouraged us to teach people in developing countries how to crochet as a means of breaking the cycle of poverty. At first, I thought the world needed something more drastic than crochet, something much more profound. That was until Stewart returned home after a summer spent in Uganda."[7]

Based on what his friend had seen of government camps and rebel armies in war-torn Uganda, Kohl decided that something as simple as crochet could change the world. He continues:

"With hook and yarn people could make amazing products. Being paid a fair wage to do so would allow them, for the first time, to provide for their families and begin planning for the future. By teaching people to crochet, we would be empowering them to rise above poverty. We decided right then that we were going to do exactly that."

The grassroots non-profit organization, launched in January 2008, now employs over 150 people in Uganda and Peru, with future plans to benefit other impoverished communities around the world. This Millennial vision of business has created a sustainable cycle of employment and empowerment for people on the other side of the globe. Could something like this have happened in your grandfather's lifetime, or your father's? Business simply happens in a different way today, with a different purpose. This is part of the Millennial understanding of what it means to be socially aware, which is a core Millennial value.

As you and your Millennial cohorts have thought and acted more globally, especially when it comes to business, politics, and social outlets, you've started building the foundation of a more connected world. Your understanding of why this global effort is important surpasses that of previous generations. You want to be connected to the world. You want to make a difference. And unlike the millions and millions of people who have

As with any stereotype, we know there shouldn't be a one-size-fits-all approach to defining people, but you should make it your business to understand and tackle these perceptions head on.

lived on this planet before you, you finally have the technology to do it.

Now, this next section may be a little difficult to get through, but it's super important that you be aware of what we're about to tell you. With all this talk of how your generation is different, we couldn't fail to mention how other generations see, and interpret, these differences.

HOW WHAT YOU VALUE CAN BECOME A ROADBLOCK TO YOUR SUCCESS

In our research for *Managing the Millennials*, we interviewed many levels of management and began hearing common stories about the challenges they reported experiencing with Millennial employees. The perceptions that follow are a result of what we heard most often from the managers we talked to. As with any stereotype, we know there shouldn't be a one-size-fits-all approach to defining people, but you should make it your business to understand and tackle these perceptions head on.

Since Millennials are an easy group to identify in terms of physical age, you will most likely be subject to stereotyping. It is a situational phenomenon people only experience stereotype threat when a negative stereotype about their group is relevant to performance on a specific task. For instance, you may hear this as you walk down the hall at work, "She is far too young to handle the Walmart account." Individuals who are highly identified with the group in question may experience greater susceptibility to stereotype

Knowing what the stereotypes are presents you with
greater opportunities to prove them wrong.

threat. But knowing what the stereotypes are presents you with greater opportunities to prove them wrong.

We believe the perceptions of managers and older workers often stem from a misunderstanding of what it is that Millennials want and value. In the following table we'll walk through the core values shared by your generation and the common perceptions of managers who work with you.

Millennial Value	How Your Manager Sees It
Blending Work and Life	Autonomous
Millennials express a desire to do what they want when they want, have the schedule they want, and not worry about being micromanaged. They don't feel they should have to conform to office processes as long as they complete their work.	
Reward	Entitled
The attitude expressed by Millennials that they deserve to be recognized and rewarded. They want to move up the ladder quickly but not always on management's terms. They want a guarantee for their performance, not just the opportunity to perform.	
Self-expression	Imaginative
Millennials are recognized for having great imaginations and can offer fresh perspectives and unique insights into a myriad of situations. Their imagination can also distract them from participating in ordered or mechanistic processes.	

Millennial Value	How Your Manager Sees It

Attention

Self-Absorbed

Millennials are perceived to be primarily concerned with how they are treated rather than how they treat others. Tasks are seen as means to an end. Millennials are often preoccupied by their own personal need for trust, encouragement, and praise.

Achievement

Defensive

Millennials often experience anger, guardedness, offense, resentment, and shift responsibility in response to critique and evaluation. They want to be told when they are doing well but not when they are doing poorly.

Informality

Abrasive

Perhaps due to technology, Millennial communication style can be perceived as being curt or rude. They are perceived to be inattentive to social courtesies, like saying "please" and "thank you" or knowing when extending more social grace would be appropriate. Whether intentionally or not, the behavior is interpreted as disrespectful or usurping authority.

Simplicity

Myopic

Millennials struggle with cause and effect relationships. The struggle is perceived as a narrow-sightedness guided by internal interests without an understanding of how others and the organization are impacted.

Multitasking

Unfocused

Millennials, as a cohort, are recognized for their intellectual ability but are often perceived to struggle with a lack of attention to details or staying on task. They have a hard time staying focused on tasks for which they have no interest.

Meaning

Indifferent

Millennials are often perceived as being careless, disinterested or lacking commitment. This is especially problematic when it comes to tasks or responsibilities Millennials don't feel invested in. Because they place value on finding meaning in their work, simple asignments like filing or data-entry can be met with apathy.

How can we summarize the 1999 sci-fi film "The Matrix" in a few short lines? Oh, that's right. We can't. But trust us when we say that when it comes to work, you'll want to be a red pill kind of person.

Willing To Adapt

It is time to make the choice between the red pill or the blue pill. You will find a lot of empathy among blue pill people who want to stay in their world of bliss in which people adapt to them or you can choose to be the one to adapt as a result of what you will learn about the matrix called Work. Reading on assumes you are willing to make the necessary changes to overcome the roadblocks that years between you and other workers have put in your way. Now pick yourself up and let's go see the Oracle.

ROADBLOCKS

Regardless of age, we can all agree that it's no fun to encounter roadblocks. They get in our way, slow us down, and keep us from getting where we want to go. They test our skills and almost always test our patience. But knowing what to expect and what to do can put you ahead of the detour. It is important to understand that, fair or unfair, you are going to face perceptions that managers and leaders have of younger workers. And although something observed does not necessarily mean it is true, perceptions acted upon *do* create reality.

Earlier we mentioned a body of research we used in the writing of this book, "Millennial Integration: Challenges Millennials Face In The Workplace and What They Can Do About Them." The research consisted of one-on-one interviews, focus groups, and several large group interventions with approximately 750 Millennial full-time employees from all over the world. All but a handful were college graduates.

But knowing what to expect and what to do can put you ahead of the detour. It is important to understand that, fair or unfair, you are going to face perceptions that managers and leaders have of younger workers.

Participants were asked three questions:

1. As a young worker, what do you perceive to be your biggest challenge in the workplace?
2. As a young worker, what advantage do you think you have in the workplace?
3. The following statement was read and participants were asked to respond: "Millennials are the most sheltered, structured, and rewarded generation to enter the workforce."

Let us briefly explain question three. It is not a common research practice to ask a double-barrel question, never mind a triple-barrel! But through the research, we were trying to see if the participants would parse out what they agreed or disagreed with or simply disagree with the whole statement. Interestingly, only four people in the entire sample disagreed with the whole statement. Responses could most often be characterized by the following statement, "It may not apply to me but it applies to most of my friends." The part of the statement that Millennials most disagreed with? The idea that they are the most sheltered generation.

Here we've listed the most common roadblocks Millennials report having at work as well as what it is they want from their experience at work.

What Millennials Want	Roadblocks
To have more opportunity	A lack of experience
To be listened to	Not being taken seriously
To be accepted	Not getting respect
To be rewarded for work	Being perceived as entitled
To be promoted faster	A lack of patience
To know how they are doing	Getting helpful feedback
To know what is expected of them	Understanding expectations
To have a good relationship with older workers	Miscommunication with older workers
To have a say in how a job is done	Rigid processes
To be recognized	Proving personal value
To know how to act	Understanding corporate culture

Though the roadblocks are fairly straightforward, we'll include a super-sized scoop of added clarity for your reading satisfaction. Want fries with that?

A lack of experience. Millennials are keenly aware that they lack work experience. They also know of the limitations this places upon them with respect to getting what they want.

Not being taken seriously. Millennials consider themselves to be problem-solvers and innovators but get frustrated when their ideas are not entertained or are readily dismissed by those with more tenure.

Not getting respect. They often experience different treatment because of their age. They talk about not feeling accepted in company culture because they are young. They are made to feel that they do not belong in important work situations.

Being perceived as entitled. Older workers perceive that Millennials want or expect promotions, raises, and recognition without having to earn it and with no regard for how others have worked their way into higher positions.

A lack of patience. Millennials have high expectations about the speed of their career development and have difficulty being patient when they feel they are not progressing fast enough.

Getting helpful feedback. Frustration occurs when feedback at work is non-existent, untimely or vague. Additionally, managers may feel that only positive feedback is desired, and if feedback is negative, Millennials will become defensive and angry.

Understanding expectations. Millennials often feel confusion about what is expected of them. They may not know how to handle the mismatch when their ideas or expectations and those of their organization don't line up.

Miscommunication with older workers. Millennial workers often experience difficulty when communicating with older workers due to technology and intergenerational differences in communication style.

Rigid processes. Millennials are more outcome-oriented than process-oriented. They see an over-emphasis on processes as restrictive to working faster, smarter, and more effectively.

Proving personal value. Millennials are impact players and want to make a significant contribution to their organizations from day one. They come with ideas and skills that are fresh. They desire to prove their value to management. They struggle with the question, "How assertive should I be when it comes to asking for more responsibility or opportunity?"

Understanding corporate culture. Uncertainty about what is appropriate at work (communication style, dress code, socializing, unwritten rules) poses a unique challenge for Millennials. They are frequently unsure about when to be formal and when it is okay to be informal.

Now let's turn the table around. In the next chart, we'll compare manager perceptions to roadblocks:

Manager Perceptions of Millennials	Roadblocks Millennial Face
Autonomous	Rigid processes
Entitled	Being perceived as entitled
Imaginative	Proving personal value
Self-absorbed	Not getting respect Not being taken seriously
Defensive	Getting helpful feedback
Abrasive	Poor communication with older workers Understanding corporate culture
Myopic	A lack of experience
Unfocused	Understanding expectations
Indifferent	A lack of patience

SELF-AWARENESS

Experts in emotional competency have suggested that the more self-aware someone is, the more they are able to control their own behavior. In our research, we were amazed at the self-awareness Millennials seemed to possess. That is what makes this book so exciting. For the most part, we don't have to convince you of what you are already experiencing! You already know!

We continue to be surprised by how much ownership Millennials take of challenges they face in the workplace. It is obvious why they would be aware of their own lack of experience, but we were impressed with their realization that their impatience affects how they are perceived. Though we were well aware that Millennials get bored quickly and need constant new challenges, we didn't know that they knew they are seen as impatient and having unrealistic expectations. Millennials are also conscious of how they communicate; they know it can be problematic when it comes to relationship building with older workers. Even so, they truly desire good relationships with their managers.

SO, BASICALLY...

You've learned a bit about what makes your generation so unique, and you're closer to being able to understand and explain what makes other generations unique as well. The best thing you can do with this information is use it to your advantage as your generation enters the workforce in record number. We have no doubt that you'll accomplish amazing things in your lifetime as a result of the characteristics that set your generation apart, such as your desire to achieve, your search for meaning in the work you do, and the fresh and unique insights only Millennials can give.

As you continue reading, pay attention to the roadblocks that await you at work, and you'll be able to stay ahead of the learning curve. Be aware that some of the workplace values you hold near and dear may be misunderstood by your older managers, but in the upcoming pages we'll guide you through the skills you can develop to counteract and overcome common misperceptions. As a generation, you've got a heightened sense of self-awareness and an earnest desire to do good. We can't wait to see what you'll do!

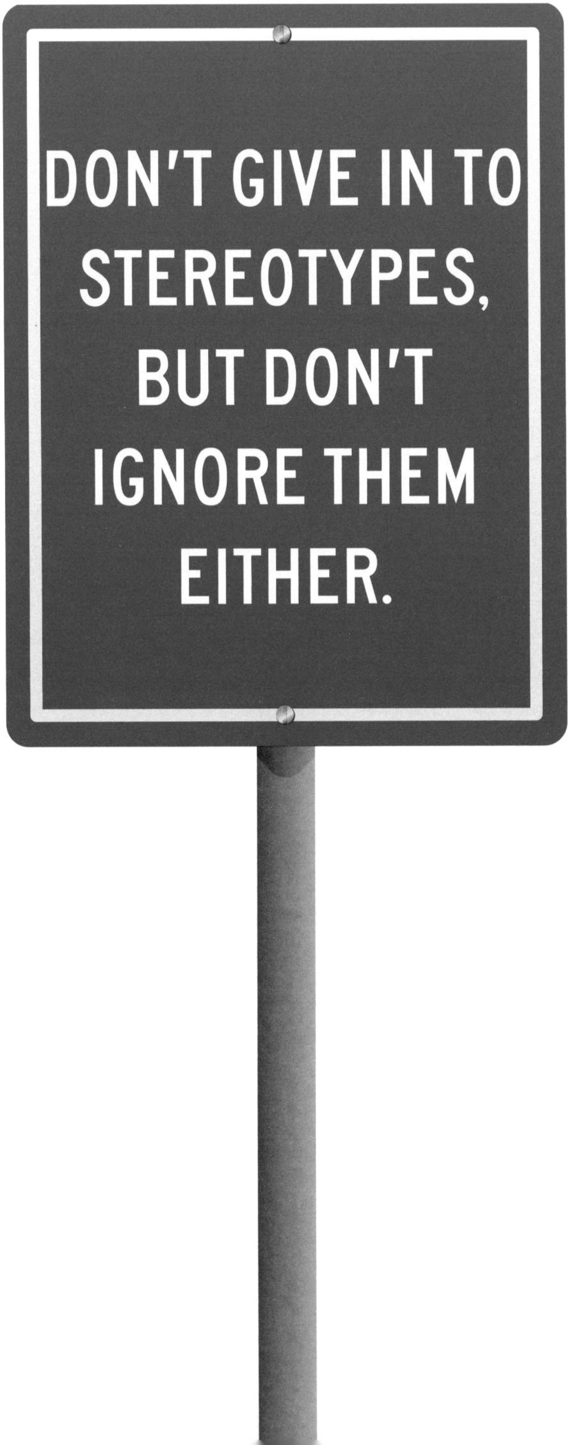
DON'T GIVE IN TO
STEREOTYPES,
BUT DON'T
IGNORE THEM
EITHER.

Chapter 2

UNDERSTANDING EACH GENERATION @ WORK

They don't work like you, dress like you, talk like you or text like you. So why on earth would older people at work think like you? When you understand the different things generations grew up with and experienced — and care about as a result — you can start making sense of things that happen in the workplace. Not only will the attitudes of older workers seem less abrasive, you may even find a willingness on their end to, likewise, understand you. But if you think stereotypes exist only for them, think again. You've got a few to overcome at work as well.

PERCEPTUAL POSITIONS

First Position: Seeing, hearing, and feeling the situation through your own eyes.

Second Position: Stepping into the shoes of another person and experiencing the situation as if you were them.

Third Position: Standing back from a situation and experiencing it as if you were a detached observer.

Every generation throughout the history of the world comes with a unique set of challenges, skills, strengths, experiences, and perspectives. These generational factors play a big role in the things we do and the things we care about. Look back just 10 years ago. See how much change has happened in the world and how great the technological and scientific advancements have been within a relatively short period of time! Now consider how much the world has changed for people who were born into it more than five or six decades ago! You simply can't make the mistake of believing that older people at work think like you or see things the same way. When you consider what each generation grew up with (and the things they care about and value as a result), you will better understand the important ways we are different. More importantly, you'll see how these differences translate in the workplace.

PERCEPTUAL POSITIONS

Perception is an often overlooked element of communication and relationships. You've probably experienced this when in a disagreement with a parent or friend and felt that you just weren't understood. Your vision of how things are is unique to you as an individual, and may be heavily influenced by previous experiences, beliefs or personal background. At work, as well as in your personal life, it is useful to assess events, outcomes or situations from a viewpoint other than your own; essentially learning to see things in a new way. We'll cover three different perceptual positions and why "seeing" a situation (or more specifically, a generation) from each of them can help you progress,

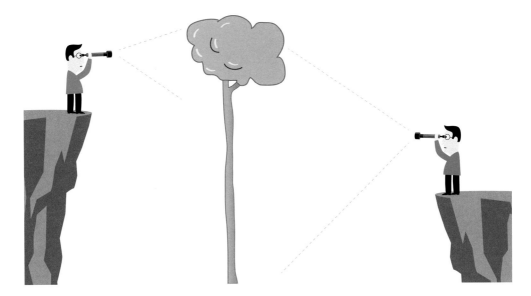

understand, and create new choices for yourself. On the contrary, failure to do so can inhibit progression, understanding, and may limit your ability to change what you can.

Obviously, the first perceptual position is what comes naturally to all of us: seeing, hearing, and feeling through our own eyes, ears, and emotions. Your reaction to and interpretation of things usually centers on what is important to you and what you want to achieve.

The second perceptual position requires you to "walk a mile in another person's shoes." You've probably heard the saying that to really understand where another person is coming from, you have to experience things as they would[8]. This involves seeing, hearing, and feeling a situation as if you were someone else. If you've lived your life in running shoes, walking through a grassy meadow in open-toed sandals would feel quite different. Rather than reacting to something based on how things seem to you, you think in terms of how a situation would appear to or be interpreted by the other person involved.

The third perceptual position is that of an outside observer, someone who is detached from the emotional element of a situation or event. This perspective is sometimes uncomfortable because it requires a solely objective view about our own behaviors and attitudes. When you try to see a situation from the outside looking in, you think in terms of observations a third party would make, what advice they would give, and what opinions they may develop based on what they see. When you gain the ability to see yourself objectively, you begin to look for opportunities to respond differently; often resulting in a more positive and balanced outcome.

Sometimes we get stuck living life and seeing the world from only one of these perspectives. We may fail to expand our vision to include the other perceptual positions. Someone who lives their life in only first position focuses on their own needs, rather than considering the needs or perceptions of others. Someone who lives their life primarily in second position sacrifices their own needs to accommodate the needs or wants of other people; this is often referred to as being codependent or enabling. And a person stuck in third position may be a disinterested or detached observer of life; always on the outside looking in, and rarely on the inside looking out. All three perceptual positions are of equal importance throughout life. It is useful to cycle through each perception as we go about our daily activities rather than becoming stuck in any one of them.

Now think of these perceptual positions as they relate to generational differences. If you grew up during the Great Depression and knew that food on the table was not always a guarantee, how differently would you view the convenience and accessibility of fast food compared to someone whose generation knew nothing different? Let's say that for most Gen Xers, food has been available 24/7, and often its origins aren't questioned or typically known. If these two people from two different generations sat down for a meal together, would their perception of it be different? What about its value or worth? This is why it's important to understand where older coworkers, managers, and leaders are coming from. The things they value, believe, work for, and expect at work are based as much on their experiences as yours are.

As humans, we share the same basic fundamental needs and wants, but there are important values, attitudes, and behaviors that are uniquely inherent to each generation.

UNDERSTANDING EACH GENERATION

Noticing the differences between generations became more commonplace with the event of the Baby Boomers. Sociologists, anthropologists, demographers, and marketers took special notice of this huge population — more than 1 billion in number — as the world's largest generation entered the workplace, changed the way targeted marketing worked, and ultimately dominated the workforce. Today, we hear about the world's subsequent generations, Gen X, Nexters, and yes, you, the Millennials, rivaling in number with the Boomers. And for the same reasons, sociologists, anthropologists, demographers, and marketers are still taking notice.

As humans, we share the same basic fundamental needs and wants, but there are important values, attitudes, and behaviors that are uniquely inherent to each generation. Let's look at what those key differences are.

The Builders (Born 1926 – 1945)

The Builders, coined the "greatest generation" by broadcast journalist Tom Brokaw, consist of nearly 60 million people. Also called the Silent Generation, Survivors, or Suppies (senior urban professionals), this generation witnessed the world post-World War I, lived through World War II, experienced atomic bombings and world dictators, and triumphed with Lindbergh's flight and the Golden Age of Radio. Due in part to difficult events they witnessed, Builders value family, faith, tradition, and community. Seven U.S. presidents came from this generation. During the 1950's, the majority of Builders came into adulthood. And though the '50s were a time of relative prosperity in America, many continued to live on a "shoestring budget"[9] and a "use it up, wear it out, make it do, or do without" mentality.

Characteristics of the Builders:

- Hard working
- Progress based on diligence and perseverance
- Frugal and cautious with resources
- Patriotic, often conflicting with Boomers who defected to avoid the Vietnam War draft
- Loyalty and commitment, especially to family, company, and country
- Respectful in the workplace, "the position is respected even if the person in it is not"
- "We" generation, not a "me" generation
- Intolerant, change resistant

The Baby Boomers (Born 1946 – 1964)

"Boom" literally describes what happened to the nation's post-war population between 1946 and 1964; more than 75 million babies were born in America during this time. Compared to the generation before, Boomers experienced greater educational, financial, and social opportunities. A larger number of men and women pursued higher education and moved away from the homes of their youth to explore outside interests. With the economic hardship endured by their parents behind them, the Boomers came into a period of optimism, achievement, and prosperity. Television, space travel, and trans-continental flight literally opened the world to the Boomers, paving the way for self-exploration, women's rights, social activism, and civil rights movements. During the '60s and '70s, Boomers experienced the Cuban Missile Crisis, Watergate, Woodstock, the Vietnam War, racial integration, Martin Luther King, Jr., the assassination of JFK, and underwent radical shifts and differing views on politics, patriotism, and social justice. The once homogeneous offices of their parents evolved to accommodate unprecedented gender and racial diversity, where terms such as "equal opportunity workplace" were born.

 Definitive reads of the 60s included To Kill a Mockingbird and Valley of the Dolls. Teens listened to The Beatles on transistor radios, 8-tracks, even portable record players. In 1960, stamps were less than a nickel, a gallon of gas was about 30 cents, and you could take home a dozen eggs for less than a dollar. A lot less. The 1994 movie "Forrest Gump" is a great depiction of the issues prevalent in the Boomers' formative years.

Characteristics of the Baby Boomers:

- Value individual choice and personal freedom
- Socially and politically involved
- Adaptive and diverse
- Unafraid to challenge authority
- Positive and team-oriented
- Competitive, often equating career and position with self-worth
- Interested in health and well-being

Generation X (Born 1965 – 1982)

In France, they're called Génération Bof, meaning "Generation Whatever." Gen Xers, as they're referred to in the U.S., get their unusual title from a perceived sense of un-belonging. As children of the Boomers, Gen X lacked

Check out the movie "Reality Bites" for a hefty, grungy dose of GenX. Top off with Pearl Jam on iTunes and a hair-scrunchie or two.

the solid identity their parents had, often portrayed in the media and by pop-culture as apathetic, aimless, Starbucks-drinking, flannel-shirt-wearing, grunge-music-listening wanderers. The magazine Newsweek referred to Gen X as "the generation that dropped out without ever turning on the news or tuning in to the social issues around them." These were America's first "latchkey" kids, the majority of them spending more time at daycare or after-school programs than at home with a parent. Autonomy and self-reliance replaced the respect for authority their grandparents had; the subsequent byproduct of the average Gen X childhood. A high number of Boomer divorces left Gen X with an atypical home life, resulting in skepticism about the traditional role of family, more caution in forming relationships, and a "do it myself" attitude. As Gen Xers prepared to enter the workforce in the late 1980s, a steep economic decline hit the United States. In place of the American Dream their parents had enjoyed, Gen X found the job market overcrowded, competitive, and tight. Because

so many adults in this generation had no choice but to move back home in their 20s, they're sometimes referred to as "Boomerangs." Gen X is perhaps the best-educated generation up until the Millennials, with almost one-third of the population earning a bachelor's degree or higher[10]. And they are raising their children to do the same.

Characteristics of GenX:

- Independent
- Resourceful & skilled problem-solvers
- Driven by reality rather than emotion
- Skeptical
- Technologically competent
- Adaptive and productive
- Balance of home & work life a priority
- Diverse background
- Artistic

The Millennials (Born 1983 – 2001)

Now for the generation you're most interested in; yours. You are unlike any other generation in the history of the world. Your parents and the adults that have surrounded you throughout life have taught you to believe that you are different, exceptional, unique, and absolutely capable of changing the world. With just one blog post and probably by Friday, you can win the hearts and minds of a small country. Yours is the largest generation since the Boomers. But that's about the only similarity you share with Baby Boomers.

Where marketers learned how to easily rope in retail sales with Boomers, you're not so enthusiastically convinced. You are practically immune to traditional marketing. Why? Because you've seen it all before! You've been exposed to products, commercials, promotions, and pitches since you were a toddler. The Millennials grew up with electronics in their hands and as a result are incredibly tech-savvy and sophisticated.

You are also the world's most racially and ethnically diverse generation. For the first time in history, there are no boundaries to where you go, who you're friends with, or what you do with your life. The speed and breadth of the Internet has caused you to be a bit disloyal when it comes to brands, fashion, and beliefs. What you think today may not necessarily be what you think tomorrow. Information is constantly coming at you and you are free to react to it.

You have been exposed to natural disasters, world violence, politic unrest, and like Gen X, you come from a different home life. Most of you live in a dual-income home where both parents work. If you live with a single parent, you carry part of the responsibility for making purchases and decisions. Why does this matter? Because you are so diverse, you enter the workplace with a different set of expectations and rules for yourself and others. Older generations don't know how to relate to you. Heck, maybe your parents don't know how to relate to you! It's true that you just might be the most coddled, self-obsessed, and "why-can't-we-have-that-yesterday?" generation. But seriously, haven't we seen your Instagram post with those cray vacay pics? Because if we haven't, we totally should …

> **Characteristics of Millennials:**
>
> - "It's all about ME"
> - Over-stimulated, short attention span
> - Technologically savvy
> - Globally connected, globally concerned
> - Socially aware, actively engaged
> - Dual personalities; online and in-person
> - Expert multitasking
> - Over-scheduled

The Next Generation (Born 2002 – Present or Later)

At the time of this writing, the official name for the generation that follows you is still up for grabs. Some have suggested as labels the Homeland Generation or Generation 9/11, in reference to the children who are growing up in a post-9/11 world. Homeland Generation refers to a nation that felt more comfortable staying home following the terrorist attacks of September 11, 2001 than exploring the once seemingly warm and welcome world. Just like the Millennials, the Next Generation (Nexters) is highly developed and technologically savvy. Information is easily accessible and, for most in this demographic, carried via Internet in pockets, backpacks, school bags, and lunch boxes.

Nexters are born into a world of convenience, and though they haven't yet entered the workforce, they will undoubtedly carry the ideas, skills, expectations, and values unique to the digital-natives, as they are called. Nexters will be incredibly diverse, racially and culturally. Migration, immigration, and ever-increasing global communication will play a key role in their development.

> **Characteristics of the Next Generation:**
>
> - Less-traditional educational background: homeschool, charter school, co-op education
> - Skeptical of political systems
> - Less emphasis on privacy
> - Seek instant gratification
> - First generation born entirely into a technical world
> - Protective of environment and natural resources

Now that you've had a crash course on generational characteristics, let's consider another key component of generational differences:

what motivates them in the workplace. We'll use Maslow's Hierarchy of Needs to illustrate these different motivations.

MASLOW'S HIERARCHY OF NEEDS

In 1943, a psychologist named Abraham Maslow introduced a model to illustrate different elements of human behavior[11]. He theorized that there are differing levels of motivating factors that influence behavior. He believed that once a person secures the basic needs of food, shelter, and water, they move their way up the pyramid to obtain a different set of more advanced needs, such as intimacy, prestige or achievement. We'll look at each level of Maslow's scale and where each generation falls.

Watch the Tom
Hanks film "Cast
Away" if you have
a hard time imag-
ining what this
would be like.
Also, if you've ever
heard anyone say
"Wiiiiiiiiilllllllllsssss-
sooooooooonnnn"
in a weird voice, this
movie would be why.

Basic Need: Physiological

The most basic of all human needs are those that relate to physical survival. Forget about thriving at this point; this is simply getting from one day to the next with all four limbs attached and bodily functions functioning. Think of what these needs would be for you. (Forget Facebook or your smart phone; contrary to popular belief you can surive without either.) This is where a person's sole purpose is to secure food for the next meal, find clean water to drink, build a shelter for protection from the elements, and establish a place for sleep. ❓ In other words, the very things that most of us take for granted day to day.

In most parts of the world, your generation may not know the need for such basic amenities, but consider how these needs may have been valued to a person growing up in America during the Great Depression. How would the drive to secure such basic foundations of life influence this person's expectations of work? Consider now where the Builders' views of food, water, shelter, warmth, and rest differ from yours. Why would this insight be relevant when trying to understand conflicts, motivations or behaviors in the workplace?

Basic Need: Safety

When the mind isn't wholly occupied with surviving, the body can begin assigning resources to secure the next level of needs: security and safety. A person's attention and focus may move to issues of longer-term stability. This could mean improving on the basics, like securing a more sustainable source of food and water. It could mean relocating from a temporary shelter of sticks and leaves to something more permanently habitable. Security becomes important too, and a person on this level may start trying to "set a little aside" for the future. The Builders did just that for their children, often leaving behind large inheritances.

Builders may be puzzled when someone says, "A paycheck is not enough to motivate me" or "I need to find meaning in my work." When Builders went to work, they were mostly focused on providing food and shelter for the people they loved at home.

Psychological Need: Love and Belonging

On this level, a person's needs are less physical and become more emotional. A comfortable home may be in place, with the basic needs of food, water, and shelter under control. It is natural for a person on this level to experience a desire for deeper connections with other people. The need for intimate relationships becomes a motivating force and will greatly influence a person's behavior. Rather than working tirelessly to survive, friendships, romance or having a family develop into one's primary goals. Maslow believed that love and the sense of belonging were just above the need for safety and right under the need to achieve.

Baby Boomers entered the workforce when there was an expanding economy and serious growth in a family's disposable income. They love titles and having old-school nameplates on their desks, as both give a sense of belonging. They are into "belonging" and have driven memberships in country clubs, rotary clubs, and professional associations. Matter of fact, they're the reason there are so many Costcos today. They love to belong! They don't get it when Gen X or Millennials don't show up for company cocktail parties or off-site meetings.

Psychological Need: Self-Esteem

Here, it is the goal of prestige, accomplishment, recognition, and advancement that motivates a person to "do." His livelihood is stable, his circumstances are secure, and his relationships are satisfying. He is driven to find something more, and so the need for self-worth, self-esteem,

The truth is, a paycheck is probably not enough to motivate you. You are entering work with a whole different set of expectations than Builders and Boomers. Though you have more in common with Gen X, they would have never dreamed of verbalizing what they wanted to the extent Millennials do.

and recognition from others becomes important. This is often where people question what they're doing with their life, and begin striving for something intangible and deeply fulfilling.

When entering the workforce, Gen X was initially frowned upon by previous generations because they were vocal in their desire for a greater work-life balance. Xers are highly independent and tend to shy away from titles and nameplates. Their esteem is tied to personal goals that are not necessarily important to others but are greatly important to them.

Self-Fulfillment Need: Self-Actualization

Unlike the other levels of Maslow's scale, this level has little to do with anyone other than the individual. This represents emotional needs, and can be a period of great introspection and achievement. You could say this is the Renaissance era of personal growth, as creativity, light, and satisfaction are at a new high. How does this relate to Millennials? We'll explain.

Compared to older generations, Millennials have had a fairly comfortable start in life, with most basic needs having been met by their parents. This advantage has allowed your peers to progress more quickly up the hierarchy of needs, reaching the level of self-actualization sooner. The result? A generation of ambitious go-getters! Millennials want to make a difference in the world, and if they see something that can be fixed or changed for the better, they'll get started on it right away.

The truth is, a paycheck is probably not enough to motivate you. You are entering work with a whole different set of expectations than Builders and Boomers. Though you have more in common with Gen X, they would have never dreamed of verbalizing what they wanted to the extent Millennials do. Turn back to pages 23 and 24 and review the chart. This is what Millennials say they want at work. You want to make a difference, and you want to bring meaning and value to what you do.

Hopefully these chapters have provided you with a basic understanding of the generations at work today. This groundwork can help you as you begin your time as an employee or seek to understand the experiences you're having as someone who's been in the workplace for a few years already. Take this knowledge and use it to your advantage, Millennials. And get ready for the seven skills that will help you rock the workplace.

SO, BASICALLY...

It's amazing how the act of understanding bridges gaps, resolves disputes, and promotes harmony in the workplace. As you seek to understand the generations that precede you at work, you'll find that in addition to what feels like vast differences, there are indeed shared truths that unite all generations, regardless of birth year!

Remember to practice and implement the three perceptual positions as you interact with older generations in the workplace: the Builders, Boomers, Gen X, even your own peers. Maslow's Hierarchy of Needs helps to explain some of the things that are valued by other generations, but nothing will replace what you can learn about your manager simply by making an effort to understand them.

The Workplace Readiness Assessment, or WRA, is a helpful way to measure your personal strengths when it comes to the seven skills you learn about in this book. The assessment is based on a research project called the Generational Rapport Inventory (GRI). Thousands of managers, employees, and leaders working in companies around the world participated in the GRI, which allowed us to collect significant data focusing on points of competency, conflict, success, behavior, and attitudes, at work.

Wondering how the GRI relates to the WRA? Good question. The research we gathered from the GRI zeroed in on the struggles and successes that younger employees were experiencing in the workplace. In other words, it zeroed in on a level of workplace readiness (hence, the Workplace Readiness Assessment!). The research also identified underlying tension that sometimes exists between older generations and younger employees. The seven skill areas covered in the WRA (incidentally, the same skills discussed in this book) were developed directly from the results of the GRI and focus on the most important risks and opportunities for Millennial employees.

Wondering what all this means and why it should matter to you? Another good question. If you've ever wanted to know whether your frustrations or experiences at work were happening only to you, the Workplace Readiness Assessment can stack you up against your peers and let you know. Is it just you, or are hundreds of other Millennials having challenges in the same areas?

The WRA measures your individual attitudes and strengths in your ability to: Build a Relationship, Ask for the Details, See the Big Picture, Know When to Focus, Go For Feedback, Be Accountable, and Recognize Your Value. These skill areas have been proven by research to be important to your success at work, as well as helping to reduce conflict between you and your managers. If there things happening at work that you're not sure how to resolve, the WRA can at least let you see which areas of competency may or may not be an indicator of those challenges.

Your WRA score is not a grade, but more of an indicator to show how you think and feel in comparison with other respondents. The scores are shown as positive, negative or zero. A positive score indicates that your answers were generally higher in value than your peers. If a score is negative, then answers were generally lower in value. And if your score was zero-zip-nil-nada-zilch, then your answers matched the average.

A final word for the research specialist/statistician/numbers hobbyist in all of us: This assessment has been sample tested and validated for acceptable standard deviation and has been correlated with data from the GRI. Personal work experience should be taken into consideration, along with individual assessment results, to provide possible areas of improved results in the workplace.

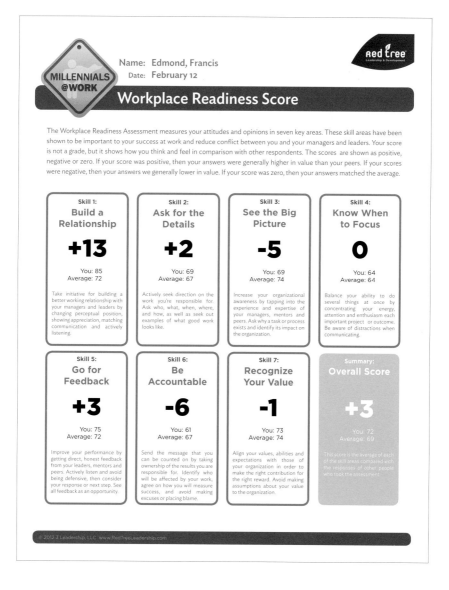

The Workplace Readiness Assessment measures your attitudes and opinions in seven key areas. These skill areas have been shown to be important to your success at work and reduce conflict between you and your managers and leaders. Your score is not a grade, but it shows how you think and feel in comparison with other respondents. The scores are shown as positive, negative or zero. If your score was positive, then your answers were generally higher in value than your peers. If your scores were negative, then your answers we generally lower in value. If your score was zero, then your answers matched the average.

Name: Edmond, Francis
Date: February 12

Workplace Readiness Score

Skill 1:
Build a Relationship
+13
You: 85
Average: 72
Take initiative for building a better working relationship with your managers and leaders by changing perceptual position, showing appreciation, matching communication and actively listening.

Skill 2:
Ask for the Details
+2
You: 69
Average: 67
Actively seek direction on the work you're responsible for. Ask who, what, when, where, and how, as well as seek out examples of what good work looks like.

Skill 3:
See the Big Picture
-5
You: 69
Average: 74
Increase your organizational awareness by tapping into the experience and expertise of your managers, mentors and peers. Ask why a task or process exists and identify its impact on the organization.

Skill 4:
Know When to Focus
0
You: 64
Average: 64
Balance your ability to do several things at once by concentrating your energy, attention and enthusiasm each important project or outcome. Be aware of distractions when communicating.

Skill 5:
Go for Feedback
+3
You: 75
Average: 72
Improve your performance by getting direct, honest feedback from your leaders, mentors and peers. Actively listen and avoid being defensive, then consider your response or next step. See all feedback as an opportunity.

Skill 6:
Be Accountable
-6
You: 61
Average: 67
Send the message that you can be counted on by taking ownership of the results you are responsible for. Identify who will be affected by your work, agree on how you will measure success, and avoid making excuses or placing blame.

Skill 7:
Recognize Your Value
-1
You: 73
Average: 74
Align your values, abilities and expectations with those of your organization in order to make the right contribution for the right reward. Avoid making assumptions about your value to the organization.

Summary:
Overall Score
+3
You: 72
Average: 69
This score is the average of each of the skill areas compared with the responses of other people who took the assessment.

Chapter 4

BUILD A RELATIONSHIP

Some elements of the workplace you have no control over, such as at what temperature the thermostat is set (this is why your coworkers bring sweaters and fans to work), Pepsi vs. Coke in the vending machine, and the speed at which the elevator goes up and down. Now, for the good news — you do have control over the single highest indicator of job satisfaction. As it turns out, it's not soda; it's relationships. And good ones are yours for the building. Stop focusing on the things you can't change and do something about the things you can. It's up to you to take the initiative for building close and rewarding relationships with your managers.

"I was a senior manager and reported directly to the vice president, who was new to our company and new to its culture. Our style and approach in the workplace were pretty different. She was quick to speak, even if she didn't know the correct answers, and frequently made promises on my team's behalf without checking with me first to ensure it was possible. On the flip side, I took the time to listen and evaluate things before acting rashly. I learned the hard way that you never want to call your manager out, instead you need to adjust to their communication style and interact in the way they want to interact. While I didn't always agree with her, I had to learn a tactful method of working together so that we could be more aligned along the way." — Jessica

If you look at the way a pyramid is built, you'll notice that the foundational layer is the largest and most important piece to the overall integrity of the structure. The foundation is responsible for supporting the weight of the remaining layers and also provides a sturdy and enduring base for years of use. Similarly, each skill discussed in this book builds upon one another to create a stable, strong, and enduring foundation for your work life.

For our Super Pyramid of Millennial Superness, we'll start with the foundational skill of building a relationship. This one skill will influence your ability to successfully implement the rest of the skills. Not only is the skill of relationship building essential to the other skills, it is absolutely crucial for finding happiness and satisfaction at work. A Gallup Poll found that employees who have a close friendship with their managers are more than 2.5 times likely to be satisfied with their job. The poll also showed that fewer than 1 in 5 people consider their boss to be a close friend[12] (someone who cares about them both at work and outside of work). What does this mean? When a dissatisfied employee leaves a company, what they're really leaving is their managers and bosses.

ROADBLOCKS

 "Anything extra or nice that I do, they act as if I owed it to them."

Millennials value attention and there is nothing wrong with that. You have been at the center of the universe's attention for most of your life until now. Through no fault of your own, you have had the baseline expectation that people are going to attend to you. Has a parent ever made a second trip to school to bring the lunch bag you left on the counter, returned home to fetch your soccer shoes so you could participate in practice, or transferred money to your debit card for an emergency? You don't think about it. It just is what it is.

Consequently, managers perceive Millennials to be self-absorbed and primarily concerned with how they are treated rather than with how they treat others. The perception is that employees in your generation are often preoccupied by their own personal need for trust, encouragement, and praise.

A manager who perceives Millennials to be self-absorbed may act as though they don't have time for you, be dismissive of your ideas, or avoid interacting with you all together. When a young woman at one of our training seminars heard us explain this concept, she exclaimed out loud, "Wow! I get it now! I totally understand why I feel like my boss doesn't like me." The bottom line is this: the perceptions managers have of your generation can lead to roadblocks.

The perception is that employees in your generation are often preoccupied by their own personal need for trust, encouragement, and praise.

*As Millennials, you share the desire to have good relationships with your
managers and coworkers. Yet, research showed that miscommunication
with older workers is one of the biggest challenges you face at work.*

The best strategy for overcoming being perceived as self-absorbed is to make the effort to
build a relationship with your manager.

Previously, we listed the roadblocks that Millennials reported having at work. On the flip side
of these roadblocks are the things your generation wants from their experiences working with
others. Here's a snapshot of that table as it relates to building relationships:

ROADBLOCK CHALLENGES	WHAT MILLENNIALS WANT
Not being taken seriously	*To be listened to*
Not getting respect	*To be accepted*
Miscommunication with older workers	*To have a good relationship with older workers*

While conducting studies and research for this book, we began noticing some overwhelming
commonalities among your Millennial peers. As Millennials, you share the desire to have good
relationships with your managers and coworkers. Yet, research showed that miscommunication
with older workers is one of the biggest challenges you face at work. Here's the interesting part:
the majority of study participants took full responsibility for the miscommunication! We saw
several statements like this, "I wonder if I'm being too informal in my emails and communication

with clients and colleagues" and "How can I know if I'm really being listened to? I feel I'm not being taken seriously because my language isn't the same as theirs."

It's not a huge stretch to suggest that every generation has different ways of communicating and a shared preference for how they communicate. This isn't limited strictly to technology and its advances on behalf of communication (think email, cell phones, texting, FaceTime), but also covers specific linguistic methods that are unique to each generation.

Think about the way you use grammar today (smh, brb, idk, lmfo). How does this casual approach to language differ from that of your parents or older siblings? And what about vocabulary? Would your great-grandmother understand your conversation if she overheard you on the phone with a friend? Are there words or phrases specific to your generation that weren't a part of her teenage vocabulary? Chances are, the answer is yes.

Amanda Grenier, a researcher with the School of Social Work in Quebec, Canada suggests these differences are exactly what contributes to misunderstandings between inter-generational employees. She states,

"Different ways of speaking exercised by older and younger people exist, and may be partially explained by social historical reference points, culturally determined experiences, and individual interpretations."[13] The fact is that every generation experiences different influencing cultural, historical, social, and technological factors. These factors contribute to how we talk, the things we say, and the different methods we use to communicate.

Cultural experiences are a huge part of the misunderstandings and roadblocks Millennials encounter when trying to build relationships. Remember this little tidbit we shared previously on page 10? Due to the accessibility of the Internet in your lifetime, yours is the first generation that doesn't need an authority figure to help you gain access to information. Previous generations relied on authority to not only get information, but also to progress, advance, and gain knowledge crucial to their success. Their success in the workplace depended on and centered around close relationships with management, while your success, up to this point, has had very little to do with closeness. In fact, an authority figure is usually the last place a Millennial will go for information. You just get online and within minutes (thank you, Google), you have what you need. This autonomy has greatly influenced the dynamics of the relationship you have with authority.

When you think about it this way, it's a perfect storm in the making. Millennials struggle with relating to authority figures and managers struggle relating to younger workers. Part of the challenge for older employees is that whether they wanted to or not, they had to take initiative for building relationships when they were younger, and frankly, they don't see you doing the same. When managers don't see Millennials coming to them for advice, direction or information, they believe:

1. Millennials think they know it all
2. Millennials think their managers know nothing
3. Millennials have no interest in learning how to do a better job at work

We've already talked about the shock Millennials experience when entering the workforce, but let us say it again. Most of the authority figures you've encountered prior to your worklife sought you out, and your perception of them was that they were wholly for you. You didn't have to initiate relationships with people older than you! They were just there, already built into your life. But just because your manager doesn't initiate a relationship with you, it doesn't mean you can't take the initiative to build a great relationship with them.

As promised, Millennials@Work is dedicated to helping you succeed at work. The commitment you make is to be willing to adapt and change so that you can successfully use the skills taught here. Essentially, we are asking you to shift your focus from what others should do to what you can do.

KEYS TO USING THE SKILL

Though it sounds incredibly simple, making the effort to build a relationship with your manager will set you apart in a positive way. In our research, Millennials who had the ability to build relationships with authority figures advanced more quickly. It was not because they were smarter or more experienced than their colleagues; they simply made the effort to interact with their managers. Consequently, managers saw them as more trustworthy, involved, and ready for advancement.

Change Your Perceptual Position

In Chapter 2, we covered three perceptual positions and how shifting positions can help generations to better understand each other. Being aware of which position you're in, as well as changing your perception, can also help you process and understand the dynamics of your relationship with managers. Changing perceptual positions is usually recommended when there has been a triggering event, whether positive or negative. In our training programs, we use a video clip from the movie "Office Space" (used under license, of course) called The TPS Report. Peter, a younger worker, is hassled by management for not attaching a cover sheet to his report. He feels frustrated because something that isn't a big deal to him turns into a big deal for his managers. By the way, the Urban Dictionary actually contains a definition for TPS Report. ❓

Negative triggering events can threaten your relationship with your manager, or at the very least create tension between the two of you. Perceptual positioning can help you gain emotional balance by looking at what happened not only through your own experience (first person), but seeing things from your manager's point of view (second person), and finally from the perspective of an objective outsider (third person). There is nothing wrong with

In the modern cubicle culture, TPS is an acronym meaning "Totally Pointless Stuff", which was made famous in the movie Office Space. TPS Reports are meaningless pieces of documentation that must be filled out but that nobody reads. As an inside joke, many cubicle workers have duped their managers into renaming routine status reports as "TPS reports" under the guise of other acroyms such as "Time and Productivity Status."

working through how you feel, what you think about what happened, or what you see in the role of first person. The conflict comes when you stay in the first person's role and only process things from that perspective. Doing so could contribute to the common belief held by older managers that Millennials are self-absorbed. It is important to learn to see things from your manager's point of view, too.

We once worked with a manager who was having problems with employee absenteeism. The younger employees felt that he used the schedule to play favorites so they would often call in sick or just not show up for their shifts. We suggested that the manager allow the employees to handle the scheduling. Understandably, he was apprehensive, but agreed to give it a try. The result was a big drop in absenteeism! Though he was pleased with this result, he was equally pleased with what he heard from the workers. "We had no idea how hard it was to do the schedule!" "It seems like you can't please anyone!" Once the employees experienced what it was like for the manager to prepare the weekly schedule, they became less critical and more supportive of his responsibility. We're not saying that in every conflict you will agree entirely with what your managers do, but it is important to pause and see things from another per-spective.

Take An Interest In Your Manager

Make a genuine effort to take an interest in your manager. Try asking natural questions to start a conversation, like: How did you get started in this business? How was your weekend? What do you know now that you wish you knew early in your career? Do you have any hobbies?

Most people are energized when invited to talk about themselves. However, we are not naïve enough to believe that every manager will welcome your interest. Some people are easier to get to know than others, so don't give up even if it feels awkward at first. If you are uncomfortable talking to your manager, try practicing in other environments until you feel more confident. Here's a great example of "practicing to make perfect" from a colleague of ours:

I was on the practice putting green with about a dozen other golfers. I was hitting a few putts before being called for my tee time when I noticed a young man walk onto the green who couldn't have been older than 11 or 12. He had his putter in hand and was working his way around the holes. I was intrigued that he paused every once in a while to talk to other golfers. He finally made his way to my side of the green so I decided to make small talk. I stated the obvious, "So, you are practicing your putting." He replied, "No, I am practicing talking to adults."

Texting and e-mail has certainly impacted the way people communicate. But it is not just technology. It is the speed at which we live. Millennials are often criticized for being curt or distracted while communicating, when the reality is that conversation has become a lost art for most generations. Author Meg Wheatley writes, "Conversation … takes time. We need time to sit together, to listen, to worry and dream together. As this age of turmoil tears us apart, we need to reclaim time to be together. Otherwise, we cannot stop the fragmentation."

Actively Listen

What does it mean to actively listen? It's more than hearing with your ears; it's listening with your whole body. Think how much you can actually hear without really listening. You know exactly which song is playing on the radio while you're talking on the phone, and even though a siren passes by and the neighbor's dog is excited about the mailman's arrival, you can tell the car coming down the street is missing a muffler. Sure, you hear it all, but what are you listening to?

Active listening is mindfully hearing what is being said and making an effort to understand the whole meaning of the message. When actively listening, a person might confirm their participation by paraphrasing what is said or using verbal signs of understanding such as "uh-huh", "yes", "okay", etc. It's important to note here that feigned interest won't do when actively listening. It's crucial that you be authentic and truly listen with intent. If you're not sure why this matters so much, just pay attention to how you feel the next time someone idly mutters "yeah, yeah, uh-huh … dude, pass the remote" while you're sharing something important.

Not only is active listening an important social skill, it is imperative in business communication. For Millennials especially, who have grown up surrounded by noise and distraction, it may be difficult to stay focused when listening. A tip to help you practice active listening is to mentally repeat in your mind the words that are being spoken. This will help you concentrate on and remember what is being said. A little effort will go a long way, as no manager wants to feel your disinterest or boredom when discussing workplace issues with you. You can also use body language to help communicate your interest in the conversation by leaning forward, maintaining eye contact, and nodding your head. By responding to the speaker in a way that will encourage them to continue speaking, you'll not only receive the information you need but help to build trust and confidence between you and your manager.

🔑 Match Communication Style

Everybody has a preferred way they like to communicate. What is your preference, and how do you feel when someone repeatedly fails to communicate with you in this way? One of the best ways to connect with your manager is to communicate according to their preference. For example, if your manager calls on the phone, call her back on the phone. If your manager e-mails, then e-mail your reply. If your manager texts you, text back. And if your manager sends you a fax, you may want to find a new job.

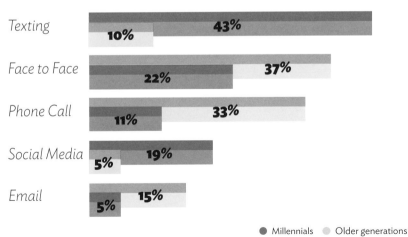

COMMUNICATION PREFERENCES

	Millennials	Older generations
Texting	43%	10%
Face to Face	22%	37%
Phone Call	11%	33%
Social Media	19%	5%
Email	15%	5%

● Millennials ○ Older generations

One of the most common frustrations among the managers in our study was the perception that Millennials don't like to use the phone. We're not suggesting that you should never use your preferred method of communication, just that you should start with your manager's preference until you build rapport with them.

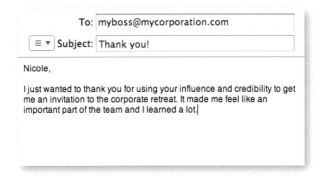 Show Appreciation

Perhaps one of the most important tips in this book is this: show appreciation every chance you get. It hasn't escaped your attention that the Millennial generation has been labeled as being "entitled." Some people suggest that yours should be called the ME Generation, claiming that Millennials are the most self-obsessed of all generations. We believe this perception exists because your generation has high expectations of what organizations and managers will do to help them advance in their careers. A manager in our study quickly characterized many of the other managers' comments, "Anything extra or nice that I do, they act as if I owed it to them."

The best way to overcome the perception of being entitled is to show genuine appreciation and gratitude when someone, especially a manager, does something nice for you. A thank-you card, e-mail, phone call, or text that specifically details what your manager did and what it meant to you will go a long way. Here's an excellent example:

To:	myboss@mycorporation.com
☰ ▾ Subject:	Thank you!

Nicole,

I just wanted to thank you for using your influence and credibility to get me an invitation to the corporate retreat. It made me feel like an important part of the team and I learned a lot.

You don't have to say a lot, you just have to say something. Silence creates the perception that you are unappreciative of their effort or that you think it's a manager's job to do extra things for you "just because."

CREATE A LIST OF RELATIONSHIPS

In his research, leadership expert Robert J. Clinton found a common denominator among the up-and-coming leaders that he studied; they each sought four types of mentoring relationships.

The first is an *upward mentor*. Upward mentors can be people who have influenced your perspective, attitude or behavior. Upward mentors are typically grandparents, parents, uncles, aunts, teachers, coaches, bosses or spiritual leaders. They may even be someone you've never met but have looked up to. They play the role of "sage" in your life. We encourage you to view your manager as a potential upward mentor; someone you can learn from and go to for advice.

The second is a *friendship mentor*. Friendship mentors are generally people who walk through the various life stages with you. They are often similar in age and usually appear in your life during later adolescence or early adulthood. You may meet them in college or early on in your career. These mentors are important because they can be a great sounding board. They are also better able to empathize with you from their own similar experiences.

The third is a *sandpaper mentor*. Sandpaper mentors, as their title implies, rub you the wrong way. They often have a critical remark to make about you when you least want to hear it. Although you should not allow them to define you, don't avoid these mentors entirely. It is important to hear and consider what they have to say. And though it may seem like they're your enemies, they're not. Keep them close to you, even if it's with a grain of salt.

One of the Millennials we interviewed had this to say about an unexpected sandpaper mentor in her life:

I had applied for a position that I was really excited about, but during the interview, the interviewer looks at my resume, pulls out a red pen, and just starts marking it up and editing it! I was fresh out of college and nervous enough as it was! After the interview, I went to my car and just cried. I knew I wouldn't get the position after how that went. But when I got home, I made the changes to my resume. I then emailed the edited version to a few friends who edited it a bit more and helped me get the resume I have today. If it weren't for that lady in that interview, I probably would have never asked for help in the first place. On a side note, resumes are now a huge pet peeve of mine.

The last type of mentoring has to do with the people you mentor. They could be younger siblings, nieces, nephews or people you meet through school or community programs. They are usually younger than you and the connection you have to them is your investment in their development. You may find that you value this kind of relationship even more than the others.

We encourage you to write down the names of people in your life that fit each mentoring category. Be intentional about developing these important relationships. One way to be intentional is to let each person know the mentoring role they play in your life. You are going to need their help to practice some of the other skills. By the way, you don't have to seek out the sandpaper mentors. Trust us when

List Your Mentors:

Upward Mentors

_____

_____

_____

_____

_____

Friendship Mentors

_____

_____

_____

_____

_____

Sandpaper Mentors

_____

_____

_____

_____

_____

People You Mentor

_____

_____

_____

_____

_____

we say that they will find you! Although, you never know … a sandpaper mentor may turn out to be your biggest fan. That is exactly what happened in this story:

Right out of high school, Valerie began working as an administrative assistant for the New Mexico Secretary of State. The Secretary of State at the time was Shirley Hooper, and she was well known as a stickler for the appearance of her office staff. They were expected to present themselves in a most professional manner, no exceptions. Valerie was born and raised in a small community outside of Santa Fe, which had the reputation as the "low rider capital" of the world. Valerie felt that people who lived in the nicer areas of town looked down on those from her neighborhood, but she was proud of her community and readily took issue with anyone who didn't see her birthplace as she saw it.

It seemed that no matter how Valerie prepared herself for the work day, Secretary Hooper always had something to say about Valerie's clothes, how she wore her hair, the way she answered the phones, even her general demeanor. Rather than this criticism feeling helpful, Valerie took Secretary Hooper's comments as insulting and felt singled out by her attention. What Valerie didn't know was how special Secretary Hooper felt her young assistant was. She viewed Valerie as a diamond in the rough. She knew Valerie had minimal experience and despite Valerie's efforts, she looked out of place working in the Capital Building.

Over time, Valerie learned not to take Secretary Hooper's comments so personally and realized her criticisms weren't meant as an insult. Valerie started taking college courses in the evening and went on to earn a Bachelor of Science degree. She worked at the National Laboratory in Los Alamos and eventually followed Shirley Hooper's advice to run for the County Clerk of Santa Fe. Secretary Hooper was right by Valerie's side throughout the campaign and was there celebrating when Valerie won the election with 88 percent of the vote! Though she had long been retired, Shirley returned to the workforce to serve with Valerie in the County Clerk's office.

Twenty years from the time they had met, Secretary Hooper was still committed to Valerie's personal and professional development. Valerie has since won two more elections and many believe she is a promising candidate for Secretary of State someday. To this day, Valerie still refers to Shirley Hooper affectionately as "Mom."

DIFFICULT RELATIONSHIPS

Okay, we know that not every difficult relationship is going to turn out with you winning an election or a spot on next year's parade float. But why let difficult relationships cause you stress, frustration, and anxiety? The end result of these negative feelings at work is poor performance, lack of motivation, and discouragement. Who wants that? Difficult relationships usually deteriorate into a destructive cycle of action-threat-reaction. Before you know it, both parties have lost perspective, balance, and the hope of things ever getting better. If you meet resistance with opposite force, it will usually end up in a power play. In almost all cases, your manager will have more power than you, so let's just say that typically this is not a good strategy. Believe it or not, there is something you can actually do about difficult relationships. Did you know that it is easier to act your way into a feeling than to feel your way into an action?

It may seem a little weird to borrow a strategy from the Japanese martial art of Aikido to help you better understand how your manager sees things, but hear us out. Close your eyes and envision that you are in the center of a mat in front of your opponent. You bow to one another. Your opponent comes at you but rather than resisting, you simply step to the side as they career right past you. The

Believe it or not, there is something you can actually do about difficult relationships. Did you know that it is easier to act your way into a feeling than to feel your way into an action?

goal of Aikido is to move with your opponent, not against them, and one of the first learned defensive moves is to position yourself so that you see what your attacker sees. This passive approach allows you to work with both your energy and theirs.

We are not suggesting that you throw your manager or try to control them. However, when you feel attacked by your manager think about what you can do to protect them as well as yourself. "Step to their side" is also a metaphor that negotiating expert William Ury uses in his work. Ury's advice is definitely applicable when dealing with managers you think are out to get you. Try these tips the next time you find yourself in a conflict at work:

- Resist the temptation to argue
- Acknowledge their feelings, their point, their competence, and your differences
- Shift the encounter away from positional bargaining to joint problem-solving
- Help them to "save face"
- Ask for constructive criticism
- Reaffirm the relationship
- Aim for mutual satisfaction, not victory

If you have tried all of the above and there is still no hope for your relationship with your manager, don't take it personally. When you have exhausted your options there is still something you can do for yourself: self-differentiate. The term "self-differentiate" was coined by medical doctor-turned-psychiatrist Murray Bowan. He argued that the inability to self-differentiate leads to a failure to grow up and take responsibility for your own well-being. A classic sign of failing to self-differentiate is placing the responsibility on others for your development as a person. Here are some signs of healthy self-differentiation:

- Staying in touch with others even if there is tension and disagreement
- Being able to state clearly what you need and requesting help from others without imposing your needs upon them
- Understanding what needs you can and cannot meet in your own life and in the lives of others
- Understanding that you are to be distinct from others, without being distant from others
- Understanding that while you may be responsible to others you are not responsible for others

Congratulations, grasshopper! You have earned your belt in relationship building. Now step out of the dojo and go kick some career booty. Or maybe just go grab a snack and come back for the next skill.

 "Grasshopper" was the name the Shaoline elder priest Master Po gave to his young disciple, Kwai Chang Caine, in the old (and we mean old) television series Kung Fu.

SO, BASICALLY...

"It's not your manager's job to take care of you. It's your job to take care of your manager." Like it or not, it's true! By building a great relationship with your manager, you'll better prepare yourself for a successful workplace experience.

This first skill may take time, and that's OK. Your efforts to form relationships need to be sincere, genuine, and not falsely motivated. The best things you can do to build relationships with older managers and co-workers are:

- Change your perceptual position, as often as needed
- Take a sincere interest in them by asking questions
- Actively listen when communicating with others, by nodding, repeating what is said, or using body language to show interest
- Match the preferred communication style of your manager, even if it feels outdated to you
- Show appreciation for the help others offer

Recognize who the mentors are in your life, and rely on them to help you adjust to new situations and opportunities at work. You'll also have the opportunity to mentor others. If you find yourself in a difficult relationship, resist the temptation to argue, consider their point of view, seek constructive criticism, and aim for a mutual resolution rather than personal victory.

BUILD A RELATIONSHIP

If you're reading this now, you either already rock at Skill #1: Build a Relationship, or you could use some help in this category and just wanted to see what was in this box. If it's the former and not the latter, congrats! But even if building close relationships comes easily to you, it's beneficial to think about ways you could strengthen your relationships. If you felt hesitant in answering any of the questions here, take some time to evaluate what you may need to do differently.

DOES YOUR MANAGER IGNORE YOU AT WORK BUT SPEND TIME WITH YOUR COWORKERS?

yes → Take an Interest

no →

DO YOU OFTEN FEEL LIKE THE OTHER PERSON JUST "DOESN'T GET IT?"

Actively Listen

no

no

DO YOU KNOW MUCH ABOUT YOUR BOSS OUTSIDE OF WORK?

Take an Interest

yes

Change Perceptual Position

DO YOU HAVE DIFFERENT IDEAS OF WORK/ LIFE BALANCE THAN YOUR COWORKERS?

Change Perceptual Position

yes

no

no

IS YOUR BOSS INVESTED IN YOUR TRAINING OR CAREER DEVELOPMENT?

yes

ARE YOU FREQUENTLY LEFT OUT OF OFFICE ACTIVITIES?

DO YOU HAVE DIFFERENT WAYS OF DOING WORK THAN YOUR BOSS?

no

yes

yes

Change Perceptual Position

Show Appreciation

no

yes

Match Communication Style

yes

DO YOU EXPERIENCE FREQUENT MISCOMMUNICATIONS AT WORK?

no

YOUR BOSS WON'T TELL YOU EVERYTHING YOU NEED TO KNOW.

TAKE RESPONSIBILITY FOR THE DETAILS THEY DON'T SHARE.

Chapter 5

ASK FOR THE DETAILS

Details, details, details. Like beauty, they're in the eye of the beholder, right? Not necessarily. Have you ever done an amazing job on a project, only to find out that it wasn't at all how your boss wanted it done? Join the Millennial throng in a giant chorus of frustration, then pull yourself together and ask for the details. That's right. You may not be able to wing it at work the way you winged it through school, so ask for more information before you start the next task. You'll not only impress your manager when you do, you'll also gain more confidence, do better work, and remove any uncertainty about what's expected of you.

"I've learned that no matter how many times I need to go back to my boss with more questions, I need to just DO IT. I could have saved myself a lot of time and effort during my time at this job if I better understood his vision. I've also learned to stop thinking that I always know what I'm doing!" — Charlotte

ROADBLOCKS

"They do not care about customers!"

One of the roadblocks to your success is not understanding what is expected of you. When you were in school, you had a syllabus that outlined expectations, deadlines, and assignments, as well as other important details you needed in order to be successful. At work, you'll be lucky if your job description is mostly accurate, and you can kiss that syllabus good-bye. And for one more dose of workplace reality? In a bad economy, training for employees is one of the first things to go. For you to succeed, you will need to take the initiative to ask for the details. Sounds simple, right? Not so much. The noise and busyness of work can get in the way of clear direction from your manager. And, as a Millennial, you will look everywhere for an answer before going to your manager. In an effort to gather details, try to avoid the following temptations at work: giving affirming nods to your manager when she gives you direction (even though you don't understand a word she's saying), and waiting to figure out what exactly it was she wanted after she's already left your cubicle.

You may be a super-hero but ambiguity is your generation's kryptonite. All super heroes have a nemesis or arch-enemy, and in this case your enemy is a lack of information or direction. Millennials value support. It is your expectation that every manager should be able to give you clear direction, resources, and valuable feedback. After all, it is their job. When we train managers we tell them that the best way to rob a Millennial of their special powers is to be ambiguous. That being said, it is not realistic to think your manager can anticipate every detail you will need to know about an assignment. They may not know all the details you need, they may be overwhelmed with their own projects, they may not have the skill set to manage or they may think you don't care.

Managers perceive your generation to be indifferent, suggesting that Millennials, at times, are careless, lack commitment or make half-hearted effort on projects they do not consider to be important. Several of the managers we interviewed used the word "care" when voicing their frustrations about working with the Millennial generation: "They couldn't care less about what they are doing" and "They don't care about outcome, they only care about checking off the box." However fair or unfair these statements might be, you may face similar comments and you need to understand how to overcome the perceptions attached to them.

Managers realize that your generation values autonomy. Millennials express a desire to do what they want when they want, to have the schedule they want, and not worry about someone micro-managing them or their time. For that reason, managers are confused as to how much direction to give Millennials for fear of being considered a micro-manager or worse, a pest. If you think about it, it is a bit counterintuitive. On one hand, someone wants the freedom to do things his way. On the other hand, he desires clear detailed direction. One of the Millennials in our study expressed it perfectly, "We want you to give us direction and then get out of our way." Couple your manager's hesitation to provide too much detail with the demands of a

Several of the managers we interviewed used the word "care" when voicing their frustrations about working with the Millennial generation: "They couldn't care less about what they are doing" and "They don't care about outcome, they only care about checking off the box."

busy schedule and you may find yourself locked in the Cone of Silence, trying to figure out what your manager wants, or worse yet, what it is you are supposed to be doing.

Roadblock Challenges	What Millennials Want
Understanding expectations	*To know what is expected of them*

In his book, *The Seven Habits of Highly Effective People*, Stephen Covey observes that highly effective people make a habit of beginning with the end in mind, "To begin with the end in mind means to start with a clear understanding of your destination. It means to know where you're going so that you better understand where you are now and so that the steps you take are always in the right direction."[17] Whether you are thinking about long-term goals or short-term projects, it is important to minimize mis-steps and wasted energy. Asking for the details will help you better understand your work, what you can expect, and what is expected of you.

If you sense tension between you and your manager, more often than not it will be the result of vague directions, misunderstanding, and mismatched or unrealistic expectations. Here is where you can cut your manager some slack. Sometimes, when you are so experienced at something, you assume everyone knows what you know. For instance, we have a friend who

Ask your parents about the old secret agent/spy comedy "Get Smart," which aired on American television from 1965 to 1970. Special Agent 86 is determined to perfect the Cone of Silence, yet the shoddy invention never quite works. Or, if black-and-white re-runs aren't your thing, check out the newer movie version of "Get Smart" with Steve Carrell and Anne Hathaway. Unfortunately, the Cone of Silence still doesn't work.

If you sense tension between you and your manager, more often than not it will be the result of vague directions, misunderstanding, and mismatched or unrealistic expectations.

owns a bunch of apartment complexes. When his son finished his MBA, he was invited into the family business. One of the first assignments our friend gave to his son was to complete a KTR analysis for three buildings he was interested in acquiring. After a couple of days, he asked his son how the report was coming along. The son said he needed a few more days but was making some progress. The conversation then repeated itself every day for a week. Finally, our friend's son worked up enough nerve to admit that he had no clue what a KTR was.

Our friend then explained to his son that KTR was not an official real estate term but an acronym he invented. It meant a "kick the tires report"; what is the price per door, what is the occupancy, how old is the property, etc. His son had spent a week on the Internet trying to figure out what a KTR was. Needless to say, he couldn't find any information to help him complete his task. He could have avoided the whole thing by simply asking what a KTR was instead of trying to figure it out on his own.

Likewise, his dad could have avoided the time-wasting incident had he not assumed that his son knew what he was talking about. Both of them took ownership for the failure, but don't count on your manager to be as forgiving as our friend was. The point is, you can help your manager help you understand what is expected by telling her what you don't know. Brilliant, right? It is a lot better than being victimized by assumption. Wow! Victimized By Assumption. What a great name for a Millennial rock band. Featured album tracks include:

- Don't Slow Me Down, Old Man
- Movin' Up Over You
- Time is My Friend, Not Yours
- Ain't Misbehavin'

Managers have their world figured out. They know what is important in their world. They know what needs to be done in their world. They know what they expect of you in their world. They just don't know how to communicate it across the Great Generational Divide.

PERCEIVED WEAKNESS

At some point, you are going to be assigned something you feel is grunt work. No matter how menial your task may seem, it could be something that is very important to your manager — or to the entire company. Just so you know, in our work with generational differences, we encourage managers to help Millennials find meaning in the everyday work they do, to help them see how their contribution matters, and to be very clear about what is expected of them. Older workers may struggle with "making things matter" for many reasons, but mostly because they have been living in their world and not yours. They have their world figured out. They know what is important in their world. They know what needs to be done in their world. They know what they expect of you in their world. They just don't know how to communicate it across the Great Generational Divide.

This may sound really weird to you, but many older managers have been trained via the "sink or swim" method. This extreme phrase refers to how children used to be taught to swim. They were simply thrown in the water and expected to learn. No lessons. No direction. Perhaps it was an effective training method for some, but the rest of us are still in therapy getting over our fear of water! We know what you're thinking, "That doesn't sound like training, it sounds like abuse!" The point is, you may have to take greater initiative to ask for the details with some managers because of "how they learned." Please refrain from rolling your eyes if your manager starts talking about the old days or how much tougher he had it than you. Just stick to your detail-gathering guns, ask plenty of questions, and prepare for smoother sailing ahead as a result of your efforts.

KEYS TO USING THE SKILL

Like we said before, the skills build upon each other. Building a relationship will make it easier to ask for the details. We promise. But in the meantime, here are some keys to help you ask for the details:

👉 *Avoid Making Your Own Assumptions*

We discussed how managers can make assumptions about how well they have prepared you, about how much you understand, and what they expect from you, but you can also victimize yourself with your own assumptions. Don't assume that you can figure everything out on your own. Maybe you are that good (insert marching band and fireworks here) but why add that kind of stress to your life (insert asprin and Ben & Jerry's here)? Don't assume that your manager knows what you expect when it comes to support, resources, and direction, or you will be victimized by your own assumptions. Victimized By Your Own Assumptions. Wowie zowie! Great name for a Millennial rival band! Bring on the Guitar Hero! Featured tracks on this album include:

- Career Quicksand
- Just Another Manic Manager
- Who Knew That I Didn't
- Stress Is My State of Mind

Managers can make assumptions about how well they have prepared you, about how much you understand, and what they expect from you, but you can also victimize yourself with your own assumptions. Don't assume that you can figure everything out on your own.

🔑 Accept The Risk

"The only stupid question is the one left unasked." What an empowering quote. It has probably emboldened and encouraged the asking of billions of great questions. It gets to the heart of why it's sometimes difficult to ask questions in the first place; we don't want to look stupid or seem uninformed. The fact is that it is sometimes risky to ask questions. We have all seen it; somebody asks a well-intended question and everyone laughs. Like the woman ordering food at a restaurant who asked the server if the baked potatoes were baked. If you were to hear this question over dinner, it would sound like a bonafide stupid question. But what the woman wanted to know was if the baked potatoes were microwaved or actually baked. Like, in an oven. Great question for anyone who loves oven-baked potatoes or *really* dislikes microwaved food. It is far better to take the risk of asking a question that may seem stupid than to prove it by doing poor work. *Or* by eating a microwaved potato.

🔑 Determine Where To Go

Obviously your manager is a great place to go for details, but you may find other people in your organization that can help you even more. Try to identify the people who have mastered a job or task that you have been assigned, and build a relationship with them. A lot of your colleagues in the workplace have what is called "tacit knowledge." Tacit knowledge is not written down. It's not necessarily rare but it is considered very valuable. This kind of knowledge is acquired solely through experience and resides only in a person's head. Think about tacit knowledge as the submerged part of an iceberg. It constitutes the majority of what someone knows and forms the underlying framework that makes explicit knowledge possible, but it isn't readily accessible or visible. The only way to transfer tacit knowledge is through relationships.

Interestingly, everyone has tacit knowledge. Think about the last time you were stuck in a traffic jam. You probably ran three different options through your head in less than a second before choosing an alternate route to get home. Because you had been there before and learned what to do, the decision you made was the result of observation and intuition. You'll be surrounded by people at work who can help you better understand what's expected of you and also teach you how to do great work, because they have been there before and have already learned what to do.

Pick A Time And Place

Be sensitive to your manager's schedule. Though well-intentioned, it is frustrating when people say they have time to talk when they really don't. When you face such a situation, just ask if there is a better time to talk in detail about your questions. It is a good idea to be specific about how much time you will need, what you would like to discuss, and why it is important. Be sure not to confuse asking for details with sharing your ideas. You'll get the chance later on to really strut 'yer stuff.

Check Your Attitude

Avoid being self-protecting when asking for details. Self-protecting is when you project responsibility for what you don't know onto your manager, such as, "You weren't very clear in today's meeting about what my role is on the project, so I'd like to meet with you." Instead, try to be self-giving. Self-giving is when you take ownership for what you know, like, "I am unclear about what my role is on the project and I would like to meet with you." Whenever possible, start your sentence with the word "I" and not "you." Unless you go Rogerian ❓ . Then you can ask, "Can you help me understand what my role is on the project?" or "Do I hear you saying I am supposed to take the lead on the project?".

❓ *Carl Rogers was one of the foremost psychologists of the Twentieth Century. The Rogerian method of discussion involves each side restating the other's position to the satisfaction of the other. The goal is to acknowledge and understand the other person, rather than dismissing them*

Questions to
Capture the Details:

What is the Assignment?

_____

_____

_____

*When will we review my work
and when will it be used?*

_____

_____

_____

*Where should I work and
where will my work be used?*

_____

_____

_____

*How should I complete the
assignment and how much
flexibility do I have?*

_____

_____

_____

*Who will use my work and
who can I ask for help?*

_____

_____

_____

☞ *Be Prepared*

We're a bit reluctant to tell you to be prepared when advising that you ask lots of questions. Why? We certainly don't want you to come across like you are about to depose a witness. (By the way, this advice also applies to job interviews.) Many managers we surveyed told stories of how they felt interrogated by potential new hires. Know what it is that you want to ask. Ask it, then allow time for a response before moving on to your next question. Try writing out five categories of questions: What, When, Where, How, and Who. For practice, you could use the example of our friend and his KTR report:

- What is a KTR? What kind of information is in a KTR?
- When is the KTR due?
- Where can I find a good example of a KTR?
- How do I get access to the data I need for the KTR?
- Who else do I need to involve to compile the KTR?

You won't always need to ask questions from all five categories, but this exercise will help you identify any pertinent details and help to keep you focused.

☞ *Write It Down*

Like you, we too are amazed by the waiters and waitresses who can take food orders, never write anything down, and still get every last detail right. Are they super-human food

Timely communication is critically important when asking for the details. So even after you've practiced everything we've said, things can still change (and nine times out of 10, they will).

service robots? The best of us may think we can remember details just as well, only to find ourselves standing in the frozen food section of the grocery store, scratching our heads and wondering why we were there. Oh yeah, waffles and peas. That's it.

When you receive details from your manager or another source, be sure to put the information into your smart phone, iPad or whatever method of note-taking and note-storage you rely on. Besides, it makes good theater for your manager. There is something magical about people taking notes while you are talking. In some instances, you may even want to ask if it is okay to record the conversation. It is a common practice when interviewing and it may allow you to better focus on the conversation. If you haven't built a good relationship with your manager, then refrain from recording the conversation or allowing your videographer to feature the conversation in your YouTube self-documentary. At least for now.

🔑 *Check In Early and Often*

Timely communication is critically important when asking for the details. So even after you've practiced everything we've said, things can still change (and nine times out of 10, they will). Plans change, budgets change, processes change, priorities change, expectations change, and even people change! Their minds, that is. There is nothing wrong with checking in early and often to make sure you still have the most important details. Unlike a fragrant mushroom or anti-social vampire with a migraine, you don't want to be left in the dark.

SO, BASICALLY...

"Your boss won't tell you everything you need to know. Take responsibility for the details they don't share." One of the roadblocks you may encounter at work is not understanding what is expected of you. What you value as autonomy, your manager may see as too much independence — and this is where the skill of asking for details steps in to clean up the mess. Some keys to asking for the details are:

- Avoid making assumptions about what is expected of you
- Accept the risk that comes with asking questions, especially when you feel like you "should" already know the answers
- Identify people and resources throughout your organization that can help you find information
- Pick the right time and place to discuss details with your manager
- Keep your attitude in check
- Be prepared; know the questions you want to ask ahead of time and take good notes when you get the answers
- Don't wait till it's too late ... check in early and often!

A little effort in this department will save you a lot of headaches in the long run. When you know what is expected of you, you're better able to use your talents to truly impress.

WARNING SIGNS YOU NEED TO:
ASK FOR THE DETAILS

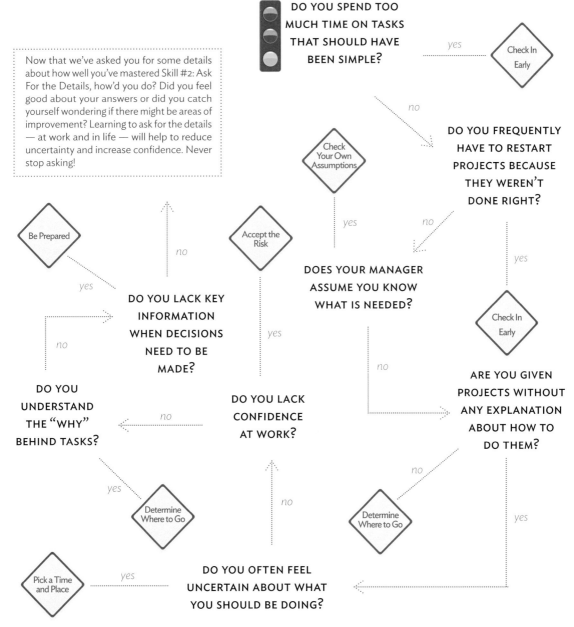

Now that we've asked you for some details about how well you've mastered Skill #2: Ask For the Details, how'd you do? Did you feel good about your answers or did you catch yourself wondering if there might be areas of improvement? Learning to ask for the details — at work and in life — will help to reduce uncertainty and increase confidence. Never stop asking!

DO YOU SPEND TOO MUCH TIME ON TASKS THAT SHOULD HAVE BEEN SIMPLE?

yes

Check In Early

no

DO YOU FREQUENTLY HAVE TO RESTART PROJECTS BECAUSE THEY WEREN'T DONE RIGHT?

Check Your Own Assumptions

yes

no

yes

Be Prepared

no

Accept the Risk

DOES YOUR MANAGER ASSUME YOU KNOW WHAT IS NEEDED?

Check In Early

yes

DO YOU LACK KEY INFORMATION WHEN DECISIONS NEED TO BE MADE?

yes

no

no

DO YOU UNDERSTAND THE "WHY" BEHIND TASKS?

no

DO YOU LACK CONFIDENCE AT WORK?

no

ARE YOU GIVEN PROJECTS WITHOUT ANY EXPLANATION ABOUT HOW TO DO THEM?

yes

Determine Where to Go

no

Determine Where to Go

yes

Pick a Time and Place

yes

DO YOU OFTEN FEEL UNCERTAIN ABOUT WHAT YOU SHOULD BE DOING?

IF SOMETHING
AT WORK
SEEMS STUPID,
FIND OUT WHY
IT'S DONE THAT
WAY IN THE
FIRST PLACE.

Chapter 6

SEE THE BIG PICTURE

Have you ever tried to assemble a puzzle without the lid? Did you know what you were building or why each piece mattered to the whole? If you are too content with the information you already have — this piece is red, that piece is a corner — you can seriously limit your potential for growth. On the contrary, when you set out to see the lid to the puzzle box (or the Metaphorical Lid you'll encounter at work!), you position yourself to create innovative answers to problems: A-ha! The white piece is a cloud, not a snow bank! As a result, you'll greatly increase your value to any organization..

"I've had managers who tell me what to do, but not why it's important to do them. I realize my boss doesn't have to explain every single detail to me, but on some of the more important tasks and projects it's very helpful for me to understand the reason for my work. I keep those reasons in mind while I'm working on my assignment." — Brian

Organizations are like complex puzzles; they can be difficult to figure out, especially for the first time. When you were looking for a job, the company's recruiting page promised, "Whether you're a seasoned professional or just starting out, we offer you unmatched opportunities to build a successful future. Worldwide, we invest millions of dollars annually in training and educational programs to build the future's greatest leaders." Sound familiar? Here comes the warning! Companies understand what is important when it comes to recruiting you. However, strategists and recruiters are often ahead of managers when it comes to understanding what you want and need at work. Here's the real skinny: most managers are not going to be like your school's career development counselors, there to help you put the puzzle together. Not only that, you may even get the feeling that pieces of the puzzle are being hidden or kept from you. But like a good counselor, we are going to help you develop the skill of putting the puzzle together by seeing the big picture.

ROADBLOCKS

 "She asked for an extended lunch hour to go shopping with friends after her third day on the job."

People who are self-aware are better at controlling their emotions, acting in ways consistent with their values, and are highly adaptive.

Roadblock Challenges	What Millennials Want
Lack of experience	*To have more opportunities*
Understanding corporate culture	*To know how to act*

You know it, we know it. You lack work experience. It is the number one challenge Millennials report facing at work. A lack of experience will be the primary reason why you won't get the job, get the promotion, get the recognition or for that matter, get the big picture. But wait! There's no need to draft an obituary of your career aspirations just yet. You have something very powerful working in your favor ... if you are *aware* that you lack experience, it means you possess the super-power of (heavens opening, golden light shining down on you) self-awareness! People who are self-aware are better at controlling their emotions, acting in ways consistent with their values, and are highly adaptive.[18] And the best part? You are far more capable of exercising the skill of seeing the big picture if you're aware that there *is* a big picture!

Speaking of roadblocks, here comes another one. Managers perceive your generation as myopic. They see your peers struggling with cause-and-effect relationships because the Millennial perspective tends to focus more on self-impact rather than impact on others. This struggle between managers and Millennials is viewed as a type of narrow-sightedness, guided by internal interests, and lacking an understanding of how others and the organization are impacted by what you do.[19] Fortunately, myopia is not necessarily a character issue. It is often a result of not being placed in a position to *need* to consider others' interests. An example of this? Your generation values simplicity, and sometimes in the name of simplicity you feel inclined or inspired to 'change things up.' There is nothing wrong with trying to make processes and procedures easier, but sometimes what is made easier for you becomes more difficult for someone else.

Another roadblock Millennials reported facing in the workplace is a lack of understanding corporate culture. Every business, organization, even small groups of people working together toward a common purpose, work around a type of culture. Corporate culture isn't always something that can be easily defined. Rather, it is learned by observation over time and by figuring out what makes Workplace A different from Workplace B. (The same steps will lead you to the big picture!)

In our study, Millennials expressed finding it difficult to understand the culture within their places of work. Among the culture shock you may experience is finding people too busy or even unwilling to try to help you see the big picture, which encompasses things like stories, rituals, myths, taboos or symbols that are important to your organization.

We experienced a great example of this at one of our training events for a company that has had great success acquiring smaller companies. The mulitnational company boasts a distinct logo and brand. During a training session for managers, we noticed a big black letter "D" hanging in the training room. During a break, we approached a table where some managers were sitting, one of which was a Millennial. When we asked what the "D" stood for, the Millennial manager replied that he did not know and that it seemed a bit out of place. The other managers gasped as if he had just passed gas in church. We then learned the image on the wall was the logo belonging to the former organization that had been acquired by this large company, and that most of the managers present in the training session had helped to build that company.

You won't find the big black "D" in the corporate handbook, the online recruiting page or on a payroll check, but it was made pretty obvious that it was something important for a manager to know about. The young manager experienced what we call a Wanna Get Away Moment (WGAM). For the record, WGAMs are not fun. At all. Think about the woman

The idea of "seeing the big picture" is really a metaphor for thinking systemically. It is the practice of looking beyond the individual pieces and to try to understand the whole.

who shows up for cocktail hour at a corporate retreat in a flattering cocktail dress only to find her female colleagues dressed in professional-looking pant suits. We know someone who showed up to do a training program at Microsoft Corporate using an Apple MacBook Pro for the presentation. Helloooo?! In his defense ... Wait, there is no defense! That's more than a WGAM, it's a "C'mon, man!" moment.

KEYS TO USING THE SKILL

Think Systemically

The idea of "seeing the big picture" is really a metaphor for thinking systemically. It is the practice of looking beyond the individual pieces and to try to understand the whole. It is an awareness that some consequences of your actions can't be readily seen, but that you still need to understand them so you can become a better contributor. But guess what? You already participate in systems thinking, and you've been doing it from your earliest of memories. You cry (cause), you get the pacifier (effect), and then there is a peace and quiet (consequence).

You don't necessarily need a lot of experience to think systemically. Actually, what you already know can sometimes get in the way of seeing the big picture. Margaret Wheatley, author and management consultant, makes a great point, "No one person or perspective can give us the answers we need to the problems of today. Paradoxically, we can only find those answers by admitting what we don't know. We have to be willing to let go of our certainty and expect ourselves to be confused for a time."[20] Author Irene Peter says it this way, "Today, if you are not confused, you are not thinking clearly."[21] It is going to require a willingness on your part to

Scientist Peter Senge is the director of the Center for Organizational Learning at the MIT Sloan School of Management. He is the author of The Fifth Discipline and a leading expert on learning organization and systems thinking. Show off your systems muscles by throwing his name around at your next science-themed dinner party. Or not.

be uncomfortable for a while as you attempt to see the big picture. But there is no doubt that you can do it.

Perhaps the best-known voice on the subject of systems thinking is Peter Senge. He suggests that seeing the big picture requires us to slow down from a frenetic pace and learn to see slow gradual processes by "paying attention to the subtle as well as the dramatic."[22] You have to become a first-class noticer. It's super easy to get so caught up in the dramatic details of something that you fail to see the little things that could help you make sense of your situation. Like in this story that happened to a college student we met:

A professor teaches a program designed for business professionals who work during the day but take classes in the evening to earn their business degree. After class one night, a student approached the teacher with a dilemma she was experiencing. She worked for a very reputable multinational company that was well known for developing a strong pipeline of leaders from within the organization. She was a 27-year-old single mother with a young child at home. She had been invited to the company's leadership camp by her manager's boss. But her manager was trying to talk her out of going. He told her that he had a huge project due and needed her assistance and that he knew she would make the right decision. She confided in her professor that she really needed her job and could not afford to lose it by making the wrong decision, according to her manager. So the teacher gave her these four questions to think about and asked her to have her responses ready by the next class:

It's super easy to get so caught up in the dramatic details of something that you fail to see the little things that could help you make sense of your situation.

1. Why do you think your manager's boss extended the invitation to the leadership camp instead of your manager?
2. Does your manager fit the corporate culture of developing people?
3. What will your manager's boss do if you don't go?
4. Which will be more difficult for you to live with, going or not going?

Looking at the first question, the student was unsure of why her manager was not the one to invite her. She asked other people in the company if it was common for the immediate manager not to be involved in sponsoring an employee to attend leadership camp. She discovered that it was uncommon. On question two (corporate culture fit), she said he was not a great manager and several people had looked for opportunities to transfer out of his department. For question three (consequences), she wasn't sure of the answer, but thought she may not get invited again and the decision to not go could stall her career. On the last question (which decision would be more difficult to live with), she said that in the short-term she could live with not going. However, when she thought about the long-term, she said she couldn't forgive herself for not taking the opportunity.

She decided to risk upsetting her manager and made the decision to go to leadership camp. It was an incredible experience for her! Her manager was not happy that she went, but it was of no great consequence because soon after he was let go. Not only that, she was given his position a month after the retreat. Yahoo!

🗝 *You Are An Important Piece In The Puzzle. But You Are Just One Piece*

We have already noted the importance of self-awareness. Now it is time to develop an awareness of others and how organizations work. A quick way to overcome a bad case of myopia is

A quick way to overcome a bad case of myopia is to realize that your wants, needs, and requests impact other people in your organization — more than you (or they) will ever know.

to realize that your wants, needs, and requests impact other people in your organization — more than you (or they) will ever know. The more you are aware of the whole puzzle, the easier it will be to find your place in it. Be curious about all the parts and pieces and how they fit together!

🔑 Be Curious and Stay Curious

Curiosity may have killed the cat but it is vital to learning. Be curious about everything in your work environment. Be interested about the work others do, too. Where do they fit in the puzzle? How does your work impact them? How does their work impact you? Do they like their job? What is there to learn from them? Remember, they have a lot of valuable stuff in their heads that isn't written down. In most cases, they are not going to approach you. You are going to have to make the effort to engage them. Try to view the people around you as informal mentors and coaches. Or, in keeping with the puzzle analogy, like a lid to the puzzle box.

Be curious about your organization's culture. Faith Popcorn, author and futurist, coined the phrase "Brailling the culture." She defines it as "reaching out to touch as many parts of the [culture] as possible–to make sense of the whole. Developing a different sensitivity to get a 'feel' for what's going on."[23] In other words, if your company's logo is a big green "S", then ask why there is a big black "D" in the conference room. Brailling the culture will help you figure out the small but important things, like who to go to for

> *"Why" questions are great but can also be tricky because they are often perceived as challenging or defiant. There is a reason why some older generations call you Gen "Why". Make sure your "why" questions are couched in curiosity, not in the form of resistance.*

institutional memory, how to dress for certain work functions, when to speak in a meeting or where to go for help with a project.

Be curious about your own work. What is the impact of your job? Where does your work go after you've completed it? Why is your job done a certain way? BTW, "why" questions are great but can also be tricky because they are often perceived as challenging or defiant. There is a reason why some older generations call you Gen Why. Make sure your "why" questions are couched in curiosity, not in the form of resistance. Practice your "why" questions with a trusted friend or family member before you set those insightful questions free, preferably with someone from a different generation.

THE FIVE WHY'S

Looking backwards is a generally used practice to better understand what is happening in the present. The Five Why's also help you find answers in your search for the big picture! The first why will determine the place where you want to begin exploring a particular issue. For example's sake, we will use a real conversation between a father and his 21-year-old son. The son's car is parked in front of the house with a ticket on the windshield and Dad wants to know about the origin of the ticket.

> **The First Why:** Son, why is there a parking ticket on your car?
> **Response:** Because the street sweeper comes on Thursdays and I am not supposed to park on the street on Thursdays.

> **The Second Why:** Why didn't you move your car into the garage?

Seeing the big picture rarely occurs after just one question. Just like trying to place every piece of a puzzle correctly the first time, you probably won't get the job done on your first attempt.

Response: Because there is no room in the garage for my car.

The Third Why: Why is there no room in the garage for your car?
Response: Because I have not moved the desk I am storing there into my room yet.

The Fourth Why: Why haven't you moved the desk into your room yet?
Response: Because it's heavy and I can't do it by myself.

The Fifth Why: Why not ask your friends to help you the next time they come over for band practice?
Response: Good idea, Dad. Can I borrow $50 for the parking ticket?

Seeing the big picture rarely occurs after just one question. Just like trying to place every piece of a puzzle correctly the first time, you probably won't get the job done on your first attempt. Unfortunately, a lot of people stop after one question and therefore limit their possible options for action. The managers in our study reported that many of the mistakes Millennials make are the result of not thinking through the consequences resulting from their actions. Generating multiple options is important to creating opportunity, but the real genius is being able to foresee the consequences of your actions. A great tool for thinking through your actions beforehand is The Consequential Thinking Game. We'll show you how to play.

THE CONSEQUENTIAL THINKING GAME

We have talked about how your generation likes to problem solve and use creative thinking skills. You're going to love this game! We'll use a Harvard Business Review case study involving a Millennial named Josh.[24] Josh has a marketing idea he has been trying to run by his manager, but his manager keeps putting him off. Josh is getting increasingly frustrated and is thinking about making an appointment with his manager's boss to share his idea. Before Josh does anything rash or out of anger, we would ask him to think of three possible options in the situation. Let's say these are the ideas Josh comes up with:

- I will share my idea with my manager's boss.
- I will give my manager two more months to set up the meeting.
- I will ask my manager why she has not set up the meeting.

Next, we would ask Josh to select one of these three options. Josh decides to approach his manager's boss because he thinks his idea is revolutionary and doesn't want to wait any longer. Once Josh has made his choice, we ask him to think of three possible outcomes that could result from the action he's decided on. Josh lists three potential outcomes:

- My manager's boss loves the idea, promotes me, and I am on my way.
- My manager's boss asks why I didn't share the idea with my manager. I could say I tried, but then my manager might think I threw her under the bus and I'll never be promoted
- My manager's boss thinks the idea is stupid and asks me not to waste his time ever again.

The next stage of the game is to ask Josh if he could accept all of the outcomes he listed. If the answer is yes, then Josh is aware of the consequences of his decision and should be prepared to accept whatever happens. If the answer is no, then we would encourage Josh to go back and select a different option and proceed to list three more outcomes. The Consequential Thinking Game is great for helping you think through the impact and rippling effect of your actions.

SO, BASICALLY...

"If something at work seems stupid, find out why it's done that way in the first place." Seems easy enough, right? But sometimes when we don't understand the reason behind a process, our nature is to criticize it, rather than to understand it. By stepping back (sometimes waaaaaay back), we get a view of the bigger picture and we can piece together the "why" behind the "what."

To see the big picture at work, follow these tips:

- See your work as a whole, rather than as a collection of unrelated parts
- Recognize your role within the whole
- Be curious and stay curious! Ask questions to learn more about your organization and its culture

In your information-collecting, you can implement the Five Why's and the Consequential Thinking Game. These tools can lead you to a grander vision of your company's inner workings as well as the impact of your role and work within the company.

SEE THE BIG PICTURE

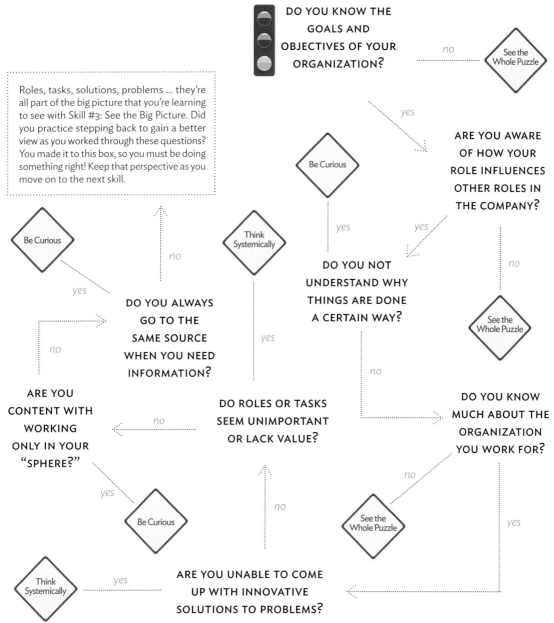

DO YOU KNOW THE GOALS AND OBJECTIVES OF YOUR ORGANIZATION?

no → See the Whole Puzzle

yes

Roles, tasks, solutions, problems ... they're all part of the big picture that you're learning to see with Skill #3: See the Big Picture. Did you practice stepping back to gain a better view as you worked through these questions? You made it to this box, so you must be doing something right! Keep that perspective as you move on to the next skill.

Be Curious

ARE YOU AWARE OF HOW YOUR ROLE INFLUENCES OTHER ROLES IN THE COMPANY?

Be Curious

Think Systemically

yes *yes*

no

DO YOU ALWAYS GO TO THE SAME SOURCE WHEN YOU NEED INFORMATION?

yes

no

DO YOU NOT UNDERSTAND WHY THINGS ARE DONE A CERTAIN WAY?

See the Whole Puzzle

no

yes

no

ARE YOU CONTENT WITH WORKING ONLY IN YOUR "SPHERE?"

no

DO ROLES OR TASKS SEEM UNIMPORTANT OR LACK VALUE?

DO YOU KNOW MUCH ABOUT THE ORGANIZATION YOU WORK FOR?

yes

no

Be Curious

no

See the Whole Puzzle

yes

Think Systemically

yes

ARE YOU UNABLE TO COME UP WITH INNOVATIVE SOLUTIONS TO PROBLEMS?

Chapter 7

KNOW WHEN TO FOCUS

Millennials are crazy-good at finger-flying texting, emailing, and updating. But you should know that your manager isn't too thrilled by these ringing, dinging, buzzing distractions. Instead of the multitasking you thought of as a strength — in the workplace, it may actually be considered a weakness. If you think your inability to focus on one thing rather than the 27 things you're doing right now is an issue for you, be advised that it is a monumental issue for your manager.

"My biggest distraction is my cell phone. Every five minutes, I get notified of something. I would be working on a project and then my cell would go off. I'd immediately grab my phone to respond in real-time with no more than a three-minute delay. When I got back to what I was working on, my train of thought was completely gone! It took at least 10 minutes to get back into the groove, but then my phone was going off again. So, I decided to turn off all notifications in my phone while I'm at work. I still check my phone but now I check it during a break or down time, or between to-do's. This has been the most freeing thing I have ever done for myself! I realized that I need to stick to my to-do list, start with No. 1 and work my way down without getting so distracted in the middle by my phone constantly going off." — Ross

ROADBLOCKS

 "Hell, I know meetings can be boring. But I'd have to hire Steven Spielberg to write and produce my PowerPoints just to get them to look up from their phone."

Disclaimer: You may not like this part! There is something you believe to be one of your greatest strengths in the workplace. But it's actually one of your greatest weaknesses — multitasking.

You belong to a generation of multitaskers, with a capital 'M' for multi. Millennials have the limitless ability to keep in touch with 18 friends at once. While eating lunch. With one hand. In traffic. And in the time it took to write this sentence, you could have sent two Tweets, four texts, and updated your status. But guess what? Your manager is — how can we say this gently — not impressed. In fact, managers and leaders across the board consider this your genera-tion's biggest weakness (gasp!). We know Millennials feel a lot of satisfaction in how much (they think) they get done in a day, and we're not here to strip anyone of their "Multitasker of the Year" award. But we are here to impart a golden-coated nugget of most valuable wisdom:

to have joy and success in the workplace, Grasshopper, you need to know when to focus and when to leave multitasking by the wayside.

As we discussed earlier in the book, perception plays an important role in how we interpret one another's actions and behaviors. Yes, your manager acknowledges your savvy grasp of technology, but the perception is this: You. Are. Distracted. And the belief is that these distractions lead to a lack of attention to detail and failure to focus on tasks. Not only that, but your manager can't get you to put away your phone long enough to talk to you about it. While your skills of multitasking may seem like something to be proud of at work, your manager's perception of your "busy-ness" may be quite different. Sure, your constant screen-flipping and task-juggling makes you feel accomplished, but is your manager silently wondering if you struggle with following through because you're just so … distracted?

Even if this is not the case, you need to understand that both correct and incorrect perceptions play a role in relationships — at work and in life. Success in these areas will require you to first, understand the perceptions of others (especially those of older generations), then to alter your behavior. This allows you to avoid feeding into potentially false stereotypes about who you really are or what your generation is really like.

Roadblock Challenges	What Millennials Want
Technologically Different	To do several things at once

It is not a surprise that managers perceive you and your colleagues to be unfocused. You blame this perception on your ability to multitask. Millennials truly believe they can do more than older workers because of their grasp of technology and the speed at which they can access information.

MULTITASKING AND THE SCIENCE OF THE BRAIN

We don't want to hurt any "I-paid-two-bills-and-renewed-my-gym-membership-online-after-catching-up-on-work-email-while-waiting-for-my-Starbucks-this-morning" feelings with this next bit, but the truth is that science can be brutal. More than 50 years of cognitive science and specific studies on multitasking have shown that multitaskers accomplish less (ouch!) and miss key information. But how can this be? Surely you are the exception, right? We'll let science be the judge!

Check out these facts, after you've finished your Starbucks and silenced your phone, of course: When doing focus work, it takes an average of 18 minutes for the brain to reorient to a task following a distraction.

 People who habitually and frequently check e-mail have tested with lower intelligence than participants who were high on marijuana.

 When multitasking, efficiency of work can drop as much as 40 percent, compared to higher efficiency when single-tasking.

 Multitasking inhibits long-term memory function and creativity.

 When forced to multitask, the overloaded brain stops processing from the hippocampus (the area responsible for memory) and switches to the striatum (responsible for routine tasks), making it difficult to learn new material or remember what you were doing once you're done.[25]

WHY DO WE MULTITASK?

Some argue that we multitask because we have to, we're just that busy. Others say they don't know any other way to get through their day. But some science suggests that we multitask because it makes us feel good; the way that washing down a Hostess Ding Dong with a Diet Coke makes us feel like we're cutting back on calories. Multitasking tricks us into believing that we're getting far more done with our time than we actually are. According to Paul Atchley, associate professor of Cognitive Psychology at the University of Kansas, we crave constant access to information because information makes us feel comfortable. But this steady stream of comfort-inducing information means that computers, phones, and devices run 24/7. We can't seem to pull ourselves away from their constant flow of updates, statuses, likes, and chatter.

Atchley further explains that "our brains are wired to respond strongly to social messaging, whether it is verbal or non-verbal. Knowing and improving our status [and] expanding [our] awareness is important to us, and as a result, information that helps us do that is often processed automatically, no matter what else we are trying to focus on." He's saying that whether you intended to be distracted by an interruption or not, you really don't have much say in the matter. Your brain is busy switching over to your friend's Tweet regardless of your efforts to stay focused on the task at hand. This is why it's so important to minimize (and when possible, eliminate) distractions while doing focus work.

THIS IS YOUR BRAIN ON MULTITASKING ... ANY QUESTIONS?

"We have a brain with billions of neurons and many trillions of connections, but we seem incapable of doing multiple things at the same time. Sadly, multitasking does not exist, at least not as we think about it. We instead switch tasks," Atchley states. Rather than doing multiple things at once (or what we call multitasking), the brain simply chooses which information it will process and goes from there. For example, when you engage in conversation, the visual cortex of your brain becomes less active, less involved. So what happens when you speak with someone on the phone and review numbers from today's meeting at the same time? You literally hear less of what is being said, because the brain has already switched back to the task that requires visual resources.

Carnegie Mellon University's Dr. Marcel tested the brain's ability to do two things at once. By mapping brain activity during a single task and then during multitasking, he showed that overall brain activity decreases when people try to do two things at the same time.

Language Comprehension Task

Subjects listened to complex sentences and had to answer true/false questions.

Object Rotation Task

Subjects had to compare pairs of three-dimensional objects and rotate them mentally to see if they were the same.

Language Comprehension + Object Rotation Task

Subjects performed both tasks at the same time.

Think about that time you were at that memorable drive-in where you ate that question-able burger. Remember watching that faulty fluorescent light overhead as you waited in line to order? The light flickered, sputtered, burst back to life, then flickered again to repeat its tiresome cycle. Literally, this is what your brain is doing when you require it to switch back and forth rapidly between tasks. Flicker, sputter, burst of creativity, flicker, sputter, burst of focus. Get the idea? It's trying to keep up with the demand placed on it by multitasking, but it can't do similar multiple tasks at once. It must choose which activity to do, then gather up its equipment and resources to switch over to do it. Then, just as the brain gets settled and ready to work — buzz! tweet! ring! It's time to switch again! The exhausting cycle continues, leaking a bit of mental-efficiency-brain-juice with every switch. Meanwhile, Millennials at work are patting themselves on the back for getting "so much done" in a day.

Cognitive scientists at Stanford University Clifford Nass and Eyal Ophir wanted to know if college students' habits of multitasking were producing cumulative or lingering effects. These students had been observed in "heavy-duty, multi-windowed, multitasking." Doubting that such

Switching tasks generated pulses of stress hormones among participants, pulses triggered by constant incoming messages.

an approach to school and work was truly viable, the scientists put students through a battery of tests designed to measure their cognitive capacities when not engaged in multitasking. Though the participants readily admitted to scattering their attention across tasks and subjects on a regular basis, they insisted that when it came time to focus they were fully capable of doing so. Nass and Ophir had their doubts. What they found, Nass says, was shocking.

The tests demonstrated that the multitaskers were unable to filter relevant information from irrelevant information, something a "high-functioning multitasker" should be good at, right? But it turned out that multitaskers in the group showed diminished mental organization skills and extreme difficulty switching between tasks, with memory function Nass described as "sloppy." Additionally, the study found that switching tasks generated pulses of stress hormones among participants, pulses triggered by constant incoming messages. Nass determined that these results were indeed the side-effects of multitasking. In a later study, he further found that "high multitaskers" had more social problems than their "low multitasker" peers, "perhaps because they have trouble paying attention to people." [26]

David Meyer, a leading expert on attention, distraction, and multitasking, explains it this way:

Big interruptions cost roughly 25 minutes of productivity, meaning nearly one-third of the work day is spent just recovering from them.

The brain processes different kinds of information on a variety of separate 'channels' — a language channel, a visual channel, an auditory channel, and so on — each of which can process only one stream of information at a time. If you overburden a channel, the brain becomes inefficient and mistake-prone. The classic example is driving while talking on a cell phone, two tasks that conflict across a range of obvious channels: Steering and dialing are both manual tasks, looking out the windshield and reading a phone screen are both visual, etc. Even talking on a hands-free phone can be dangerous," he says. *"If the person on the other end of the line is describing a visual scene — say, the layout of a room full of furniture — that conversation can actually occupy your visual channel enough to impair your ability to see what's around you on the road.*

With a note of warning, Meyer adds that "when you add up all the leaks from these constant little switches, soon you're hemorrhaging a dangerous amount of mental power." Theorist Linda Stone has defined multitasking as paying "continuous partial attention." She suggests that employees generally don't stick with a single task for more than several minutes at a time. And, when left uninterrupted, she says that people simply find ways to interrupt themselves. Stone reports that big interruptions cost roughly 25 minutes of productivity, meaning nearly one-third of the work day is spent just recovering from them. She also estimates that office workers keep around eight windows open on their computer screens throughout the day and flip between them an average of every 20 seconds. Does this sound like anyone you know? This growing epidemic of task-switching and page-jumping has caused the American Journal of Psychiatry to add "Internet addiction" to its Diagnostic and Statistical Manual of Mental Disorders, making the need to constantly be online a bonafide disorder right up there with schizophrenia.[27]

THE FOCUS/ENERGY MATRIX

In the 1990s, business professors Heike Bruch and the late Sumantra Ghoshal conducted some in-depth research on energy and focus and how the two relate to personal productivity. Their studies resulted in a frequently-referred to model, The Focus/Energy Matrix. The graphic below shows the professors' findings. Each section or square of the graphic shows a different level of focus and energy among workers. See if you can identify yourself in any of them!

The Procrastinators (Low Energy / Low Focus)

When you're done putting off that last load of laundry, check out this statistic: procrastinators make up 30 percent of the workforce! Though they usually perform the tasks that are required of them — going to meetings, responding to communication, etc. — they rarely take initiative or put themselves to work to drive results. Most procrastinators need constant attention, prodding, reminding, and well, nagging. Here's a bit of free advice: Try not to be a part of this percentage.

The Disengaged (High Focus / Low Energy)

20 percent of workers fall in this category. People with high focus and low energy dive into single issues, working through tasks one thing at a time, and may feel overwhelmed if multiple demands are placed on their time or have additional projects added to their to-do lists. Some have a hard time committing to projects or duties that don't feel important. With low energy levels, the disengaged worker suffers from burnout far more often than their peers. In this case, the person is doing the right thing in terms of focus, but lacks the energy to engage with their work.

The Distracted (Low Focus / High Energy)

Short-sighted, overcommitted, full of good intentions (the highest-populated group of study participants at 40 percent!) most people fall into this category. If these traits sound familiar, then you or someone you know at work could be distracted. (Hey! A squirrel!) Projects tend to get done, but not always with the best effort or promised results. Sometimes there is the expectation at work to "look busy", and this group of workers falls prey to that pressure by taking on more than is realistic and keeping up the appearance of having too much to do.

The Purposeful (High Focus / High Energy)

Purposeful employees — the smallest group at only 10 percent — stay focused and energized not only in the midst of crisis, but even after the dust has settled. Time and energy are planned and spent carefully and are protected from distractions. Rather than focusing on checking boxes or crossing tasks off lists, focus is on overall outcome and achievement. These workers are skilled at finding ways to reduce stress and effectively balance worklife with hobbies and outside interests. And unlike the other three categories, people in this one welcome new opportunities and actively pursue new goals. Want another bit of free advice? DO try to be a part of this percentage.

KEYS TO USING THE SKILL

During any given day anywhere in the world, all kinds of work is being done. Some work happens by reacting or responding to requests. Some work is done by solving problems and diffusing situations. Other work hinges on communication with people, and some work requires the creation of something new. Studies have shown that for the type of work that requires creativity (an upper-brain function), the overall quality of work is greatly reduced by distractions. By knowing when to remove distractions from your work day so that you can focus, you'll give your best effort to important work and communication.

But for Millennials who have grown up living la vida multitasking, how do you suddenly learn to focus? You start by weaning yourself from Facebook for minutes, then half-hours, then hours, and also implement the following helpful tips.

Sort & Prioritize : Separate Activities into Focus Work and Responsive Work

Not everything you do in the course of a day requires laser-like focus, and there will be times when responding to requests and completing tasks simultaneously will be more important than using your newly-acquired mad focusing skills. But you'll need to be clear on which situation calls for which type of work. It's helpful to divide your work responsibilities into two groups: Focus and Responsive.

Focus Work: Focus work is what it implies, work that requires focus. Think of focus work as what happens when a series of decisions needs to be made in order to accomplish a larger task. Some examples of focus work are:

Focus Work:

- Problem solving: forecasting, supply and demand chains, budgets, strategies, detailed reports
- Writing: marketing collateral, web copy, press releases, email campaigns, proposals, reviews
- Designing: graphics, web building, logos, marketing campaigns, new product images
- Creating: concept creation, prototyping, adapting products to demands, marketing strategy

---

When you find tasks like these on your to-do list, put your cell phone away (on silent mode, please) and quit your email program. One way to handle the interruptions that will inevitably pop up is to ask if you can respond later, using discretion to identify high-priority interruptions from those that can wait. Remember that you can avoid being your own worst enemy by removing the distractions within your control and diffusing those that are not.

Responsive Work: Responsive work permits you to be responsive, as in "the virtual door to my online house is open, come on in." This kind of work allows more room for interruptions and distractions because it doesn't require your strict attention. Think of responsive work as what happens when you make singular decisions, such as transferring a phone call to the correct department. Some examples of responsive work are:

Responsive Work:

- Monitoring: overseeing studies or experiments, testing, security
- Processing: programming, running reports, updating systems
- Data entry: entering orders, addresses, responses, etc.
- Receptionist: answering phone calls and questions, receiving mail and deliveries, e-mails

---

In these situations, it's probably okay to have a few screens open in the background while you do your work. Be careful not to find reasons for why all your work should fit into this category, but do allow yourself to be responsive to texts, IMs, phone calls, and other opportunities to reconnect with people following distraction-free work time. When you've had your head buried in a huge project all morning, it can be a welcome and needed break to divert your

Focus Work:

_____

_____

_____

_____

_____

_____

_____

_____

_____

Responsive Work:

_____

_____

_____

_____

_____

_____

_____

_____

_____

_____

_____

No one should be expected to "focus, focus, focus!" 24 hours a day, but it is imperative that you learn how to manage and control your ability to focus when you need to.

attention to something relaxing, entertaining or personal before diving back in.

🔑 Schedule Distraction-free Time for Focus Work

The biggest challenge with focus work is not that it takes time to do it well, but that distractions will cause you to stop.start.stop.start. In fact, when a distraction (such as hearing a familiar voice down the hall or a text popping up on your phone) interrupts a steady stream of focused, intent work, your brain has recognized and registered the interference long before you do. Even if you glance at your phone without responding to the message, it's too late. Your mind stopped focusing the second it registered the recognizable sound of a friend or incoming text. This constant on-off flipping of the concentration switch gets in the way of (and usually halts) good, productive work.

No one should be expected to "focus, focus, focus!" 24 hours a day, but it is imperative that you learn how to manage and control your ability to focus when you need to. There's a reason your concentration turns on and off; your mental health and relaxation depend on it. So, know when your work requires focus and schedule time to remove as many distractions as possible.

A suggestion for the Millennial multitasker: let people know you'll be taking some time for focus work. This includes notifying those you work with as well as your legions of FB fans. Then, commence tackling tasks one at a time. Stick with the first item on your list until it's done, if possible. If you find your attention teetering on the rope (on average, this takes just under 20 minutes — with or without an umbrella), move on to the next item of business. Write a sticky note or send yourself a message about where you left off so you know where to pick up later on. Then, with your concentration safely balancing above, give the next task your complete attention. Again, focus on what you're doing for as long as you can.

Perhaps the most simple instruction we can give is this: do what you're doing with 100% focus until you're done. Then, move on. To make the best progress on work that requires focus, plan for distraction-free time to complete your projects. Minimize distractions (this means you, YouTube), focus, and git'er done.

🔑 Always Communicate Distraction-Free

Commit right now (do we hear an Amen?) to begin communicating without distractions. Studies have shown that texting, browsing the Web or doing something else while communicating dramatically affects your ability to participate in, let alone comprehend, conversation. In fact, a university study showed that texting while having a verbal conversation lowers a person's comprehension below that of the legally drunk level, and in some cases, is equal to not having participated in the conversation at all.

Try to recall the last time you talked to someone while they played DrawSomething or shopped for Italian leather boots online. Did you have to ask if they were listening? What happened to your perception of the other person if you had to repeat yourself once? How 'bout twice? This is precisely why the skill of knowing when to focus is crucial in your work environment. What image did you convey by asking your manager to repeat their question at yesterday's strategy meeting because you were busily texting about last night's totes rad party? Not a very good one, huh?

Do yourself (and your coworkers and your career) a huge favor. When you are communicating, communicate. Don't text. Don't Tweet. Don't update. Don't play Words. Just, communicate.

It will become easier with practice and you will avoid giving the wrong impression to those you communicate with.

And if you need one last solid reason to communicate without distraction, consider this: if you fail to focus on the words you speak and the words that are spoken to you, you are actually perpetuating and slipping into the single largest stereotype your managers have of you as a Millennial. We don't know how this makes you feel, but here's our two-cents — there's nothing worse than being stereotyped until you realize you *are* the stereotype.

SO, BASICALLY...

"Sometimes multitasking will be your greatest weakness. And your boss's greatest pet peeve." Though you see your multiple open computer windows as a way of getting more done, your boss sees it differently. You say "productive" ... he says "distracted."

Science has shown that multitasking doesn't really exist. At least, not in the way we think it does. The brain can't really handle the constant switching back-and-forth that multitasking demands, and studies prove that our work suffers greatly when we try to do too much at once. The solution? Know when to focus. Keys to using this skill include:

- Sort and prioritize your work by separating activities into focus work and responsive work
- Schedule blocks of distraction-free time for focus work
- When communicating, remove outside distractions

The Focus/Energy Matrix offers a way to identify where you may fall in your ability to focus and level of energy at work. Strive to land in the High Focus/High Energy category, where time and energy are spent carefully and protected from distractions.

KNOW WHEN TO FOCUS

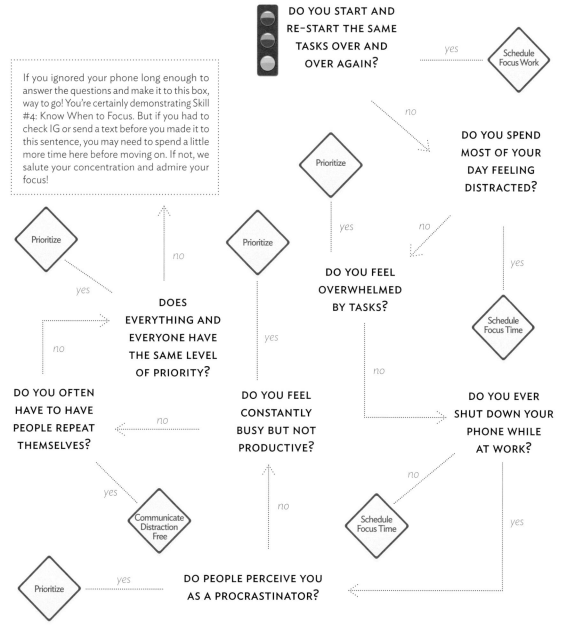

DO YOU START AND RE-START THE SAME TASKS OVER AND OVER AGAIN?

yes — Schedule Focus Work

no

If you ignored your phone long enough to answer the questions and make it to this box, way to go! You're certainly demonstrating Skill #4: Know When to Focus. But if you had to check IG or send a text before you made it to this sentence, you may need to spend a little more time here before moving on. If not, we salute your concentration and admire your focus!

DO YOU SPEND MOST OF YOUR DAY FEELING DISTRACTED?

Prioritize

yes   *no*

Prioritize

yes

DO YOU FEEL OVERWHELMED BY TASKS?

Prioritize

no

Schedule Focus Time

yes

yes

no

DOES EVERYTHING AND EVERYONE HAVE THE SAME LEVEL OF PRIORITY?

yes

no

DO YOU OFTEN HAVE TO HAVE PEOPLE REPEAT THEMSELVES?

no

DO YOU FEEL CONSTANTLY BUSY BUT NOT PRODUCTIVE?

DO YOU EVER SHUT DOWN YOUR PHONE WHILE AT WORK?

no

yes

Communicate Distraction Free

no

Schedule Focus Time

yes

Prioritize

yes

DO PEOPLE PERCEIVE YOU AS A PROCRASTINATOR?

YOUR MISTAKES WILL OFTEN BE MORE VALUABLE THAN YOUR SUCCESSES.

Chapter 8

GO FOR FEEDBACK

Let's face it, team. Getting a ribbon just for showing up on the field wasn't the best preparation for today's competitive workplace. If your coaches and parents had nothing but nice things to say about how well you warmed the bench at every Little League game, you may not be ready for your manager's blunt review of your performance. But if you fail to accept constructive criticism or don't use it as a tool to improve, you will distance yourself from the people who are in a position to help you. When you go for feedback, you demonstrate that you are willing to learn. The reward? You accelerate the development of your career and just might learn a few valuable things along the way.

"At one of my jobs I was ignored by my boss for more than three years. I've also had jobs where I received nothing but criticism. Critical feedback doesn't have to be harsh, but being told that you are doing well if you are not is much worse than receiving feedback that's hard to hear. It doesn't bruise my ego to admit we all have things we can improve." — Paul

ROADBLOCKS

" If you correct them, they will quit."

A huge frustration Millennials share is not only the lack of timely feedback, but the absence of helpful feedback. You have grown up in a faster-paced world than generations before you. Whether shopping online, applying for a job, ordering a burrito or getting approval for a loan, you expect an immediate response to your requests. With that fast pace in mind, Millennials often interpret a lack of feedback as simply being ignored — a feeling you are not super used to. If you do receive feedback, it is often times delivered in a way that is uncomfortable (meaning, no fluffy sugar coating) and hard to accept. You thrive on feedback that you perceive as positive because you place a great amount of value on achievement.

It is the intrinsic value of achievement that drives the Millennial need to be affirmed. It's not that you *need* to achieve as much as that you *have* to achieve. You not only have high expectations of yourself, but there are many people who expect their investment in you to pay off. Many Millennials have parents who paid trainers big money so their little pride-and-joys (that's you) could excel at hitting a baseball, dribbling a basketball, kicking a soccer ball, tickling the ivories, digging out a volleyball, diagramming a sentence, identifying an obtuse angle or balancing on a high beam. There's a lot riding on your success! Couple that investment with the pressure of not being allowed to fail and it's easy to understand why you may push back a bit when you receive feedback you consider to be negative.

That same pushback — even if an honest result of your desire to achieve — is perceived by managers as the Millennial trait of defensiveness. Managers who thought they were giving helpful feedback to Millennial employees told us about the common reactions they experienced; Millennials seemed angry, guarded, offended, resentful, and disagreeable when presented with critique and evaluation. Many managers choose the easier option of simply not giving feedback, rather than subjecting themselves to the drama that ensues. And so our theme continues! But before you give up, there are several things you can do when you feel like you are not getting helpful feedback.

Roadblock Challenges	What Millennials Want
Getting helpful feedback	*To know how they are doing*

IF MANAGERS DON'T COME TO YOU, GO TO THEM

Back in the day when Scooby Doo was just a pup, feedback was only to be initiated by a manager. When a manager had something to say, you got feedback. Otherwise, you didn't. More often than not, feedback was emotionally triggered. (Usually not a good thing for the person on the receiving end!) Ken Blanchard, co-author of *The One Minute Manager,* calls this kind of feedback 'Seagull Management.' In his words, "They fly in, crap all over you, and fly out." For those of you who telecommute or work in virtual environments, be sure to invest in a good, strong umbrella. While there are a lot of great perks to working remotely, one downside is not receiving good feedback from your manager.

Fortunately, over the past couple of decades, there has been a shift in thinking about the feedback process. A lot of research has been done about the concept of Feedback Seeking Behavior

(FSB). Changes in the school of thought surrounding FSB mean that the feedback process can be initiated by you: more often, on your schedule, and on the basis of your needs. It is totally acceptable for you to ask for feedback. Especially if you are new to a task or organization. Going for feedback is a proactive strategy that can help develop your ability, improve your performance, and also enhance your creativity.[28]

Studies show that when people ask for feedback, it helps them to reduce ambiguity and uncertainty about what to do at work. It can also help you understand how your behaviors are evaluated.[29] Remember, as a Millennial, ambiguity is your kryptonite. Feeling unsure about how you are doing at work can lead to stress, which can negatively affect your physical and mental health, your ability to control emotions, and your future performance.

In Chapter 4, we talked about asking for the details. When you use the skill of gathering details, it helps you understand the "what" of your job, like: What is expected? What does success look like? What are my resources? What is the top priority? This type of information gathering is called process feedback. Going for feedback is a different type of information seeking, referred to as performance feedback. It means taking the initiative to seek out evaluation on the work you have already completed, more like the "how" of your job: How did I do? How could I do it better? Or, if you're feeling cheeky, how do you like me now?

Both kinds of feedback serve as a pressure valve to prevent frustration and anger from building up between employees and those responsible for giving feedback. Many of the Millennials in our study struggled with the question, "If I am always going for feedback is there a point where I become a nuisance to my manager?" The last thing you want is for your manager to avoid you, go silent on you or leave you wondering what-on-earth she's thinking. But you don't necessarily need to limit your feedback-giving audience to just your manager. Peers, mentors, and other employees can serve as a great source of feedback. Look for people who are approachable, accessible, and have expertise in the area in which you're gathering information. People who seek feedback for personal improvement are more likely to select those with task expertise rather than those with power.

Research shows that people who make the effort to go for feedback tend to work more efficiently, are happier on the job, stay with their organizations longer, and are better performers than those who don't.

Research shows that people who make the effort to go for feedback tend to work more efficiently, are happier on the job, stay with their organizations longer, and are better performers than those who don't.[30] Conversely, those reluctant to seek the kind of feedback that will help them improve are poor performers. Also, the better the performer you are, the more well-received your request for feedback will be. Hmmm, if going for feedback will make you a better performer, a happier worker, and a more valued employee, then why hesitate? Go on! Go for feedback, you rock star of an employee, you!

Actually, there are many good reasons why a person would be reluctant to go for feedback. One is the fear of what you may hear. Nobody likes receiving critical or negative feedback in the moment, even if it eventually leads to better things. Another reason is the feedback you receive can sometimes be confusing or not at all what you expected. This can happen when the person giving feedback is distracted, hurried or altogether uninvested (or uninterested) in your progress.

Perhaps the biggest reason people avoid seeking feedback is that it can be downright demoralizing and embarrassing. We're not going to say it isn't, so yes, your fears are legit. But the upside

The key is to focus first on improving your ability rather than proving your ability. Proving your ability has its place and is important, but it will come more naturally after you've improved your ability.

of going for feedback is far greater than the downside. It can give you a true picture of how you are doing, it can be validating, and it shows that you really care about doing a great job.

We mentioned that poor performers are less likely to go for feedback. Usually this is because they are worried about making a negative impression on their managers. They worry they may be perceived as lacking confidence or having insecurity about their ability. If you find yourself in this mindset, think about having a distinct goal when you seek feedback. Don VandeWalle, Chair of the Management and Organizations Department in the Cox School of Business at Southern Methodist University, suggests two goals that drive asking for feedback: learning goals and performance goals. He explains the difference this way — people with learning goals focus on improving their ability, while people with performance goals focus on proving their ability.[31]

VandeWalle points out that individuals with a learning orientation try harder to seek feedback when they are overwhelmed by a task or think they lack the ability to do the task. He also suggests that individuals with a learning goal orientation seek feedback sooner after unfavorable events than individuals with a performance goal orientation do. The key is to focus first on improving your ability rather than proving your ability. Proving your ability has its place and is important, but it will come more naturally after you've improved your ability. More on proving your ability later on, in Chapter 9.

Even people who worked in their positions for years had questions about what they should be doing or how they were doing! The moral? Don't let yourself be held back with the worry of what people will think if you go for feedback.

Another strategy for seeking feedback is to simply monitor and observe your environment to learn from other people's actions, conversations, mistakes, and successes. It is what leadership guru Warren Bennis calls being a "first class noticer." Monitoring is somewhat like the skill of seeing the big picture. It is the practice of observing actions or cues that may not even be directed at you, but certainly can help you grow in your ability and success at work.

KEYS TO USING THE SKILL

Now that you're a locked-and-loaded feedback-seeker, we want to help buffer the risks of actually doing it! Let's look at the obstacles that could lie in your path when asking for feedback.

Social Expectations

Susan J. Ashford, a researcher with Dartmouth College, completed her dissertation about feedback-seeking within organizations. She observed that individuals most commonly asked for feedback on important issues, in new or uncertain situations or when they felt they were failing to meet goals or expectations. On the other hand, employees who had been with a company or organization for longer periods of time rarely went for feedback. She observed this reluctance was based on social pressure that the tenured employees felt to appear confident or self-assured.[32] What is the irony in Ashford's findings? Even people who worked in their positions for years had questions about what they should be doing or how they were doing! The moral? Don't let yourself be held back with the worry of what people will think if you go for feedback.

In the end, it's the people who ask for feedback, gather new information, and build on what they learn who go on to accomplish great things.

Imagine how many thousands of questions go unanswered every day, how much uncertainty is felt at work or how much information is withheld because some employees feel they have to appear confident and self-assured in front of their peers. Don't let that be you! It sounds silly, but it's impossible to know what you don't already know, right? And what better way to know something you don't already know than to ask! There's nothing wrong with wanting to know how you're doing at work. On the contrary, your going for feedback should only be evidence of your desire to do well and succeed. In the end, it's the people who ask for feedback, gather new information, and build on what they learn who go on to accomplish great things.

🔑 Relationship Quality

When there's something you need, say, a ride to the airport, an honest opinion about today's wardrobe choice or an editing pass on a crucial report, who do you turn to? Do you typically go to the person you're least close to for help? Or do you seek out a trusted friend, a close colleague or sibling? Usually when we reach out, we do so with the people we trust and feel close to. Most of the time, it should be the same when going for feedback. Occasionally, you may need to approach a distant manager or unknown department for specific feedback. But let's just say that as a general practice, you'll go to the people you trust.

This is where we circle back to the first skill of building a relationship. As you make the effort to get to know your managers and coworkers, when it's your time to ask for help — you'll get it. Now do you see the importance of building those close relationships at work? You'll get more honesty, more time, and more investment on the part of your employers as you build relationships with the people who can help you the most.

🔑 Choose the Right Medium for Feedback

Do you remember earlier on when we talked about matching communication style with your manager? If they text with a question, text your reply. If they email with an important matter, email your response. Of course when going for feedback, you still want to be respectful of the other person's preferred method of communication, but there is a catch that makes feedback-seeking a bit of an exception.

Have you ever received an IM or text from someone and weren't totally sure how they meant the message? Like, was it a joke, was it sarcasm or were they being serious? It's hard to gauge what was really said when you're unsure of how something was really meant. That's the problem with going for feedback via email or text. You can't hear their tone of voice or see their facial expressions, both of which are clues that can tell you more of the story. Obviously, there will be situations when timing is of greater importance than the movement of your manager's eyebrows or their impressive range of vocal pitch, so use good judgement to determine when to reach out for feedback in other ways. That being said, aim for face-to-face time when going for feedback (it's similar to FaceTime, but sans iPad), and leave the texting and emailing for less ambiguous matters.

🔑 Don't Be a Mind Reader. At Least, Not While You're at Work

Here's a familiar scene from just about any chick-flick: Guy likes Girl. Girl doesn't like Guy. Guy doesn't know it. Guy leans in for kiss. Girl pulls back in horror. Awkward moment ensues. Guy likes New Girl. Girl realizes in flash of discovery that she likes Guy! Really, really likes Guy! Guy doesn't know it. Girl and New Girl have conflict over Guy. Awkward moment ensues.

While usually not as dramatic as a rehearsed and scripted scene from a movie, equally awkward moments happen at work when we try to read minds and act on what we think we know about a project, task or responsibility.

Here's a real life case-in-point from Carly, a Millennial employee:

A few years ago, I accepted an internship as Art Director for an ad agency. It was my first time working in a professional setting and I was excited to show how much I had learned in school and how well I could do my job. My first assignment was to design a template to be used for the company's newsletter. My boss gave me a few images to work with and a deadline and that was it ... I was on my own to design with no direction and no examples. I took this to mean that I had full creative license. No one checked in with me and I didn't check in with anyone. It was really fun! I worked for hours on the project and after a few days, had five different templates to show my boss. I was so excited for him to see my work, I knew he would be impressed that I had taken such initiative. Up to this point, no one had seen what I was working on. The day came to show him the new templates, and I anxiously awaited for what was sure to be praise for a job well-done. That's not what happened at all.

Awwwwwkward. Carly continues:

When my boss saw the templates, he told me they weren't at all what he needed. He kept asking me if I didn't understand the project and wanted to know why I hadn't been checking in. I told him that I did the best I could according to the (lack of) direction I had received, and that I thought this was my project to work on. All he could say was 'Why didn't you just check in?'. I felt about two-feet tall, but I learned my lesson.

🔑 Stick to the Task (and Feedback) at Hand

While it may be killing you to know what your boss really thinks of your new (and slightly ostentatious) bow tie or hair color, be sure to respect their time by asking for feedback that is relevant to the task or situation at hand. How do you accomplish this, you ask? Make sure you have clearly communicated what the task or situation at hand is! This way, the time you spend together can be productive and beneficial to both of you. And more importantly, the feedback you receive can be as relevant and helpful as possible.

Managers are people too, prone to moods and bad days just like you, and they're not always on their A-game.

Your Manager's Mood

This is where monitoring can be very helpful. Pay attention to when, where, and how other people approach your manager. As an example, Gen Xers are great to observe if you're trying to understand how to work with Baby Boomers. Wondering when is the right time to pitch an idea to your boss or want to ask their opinion on something? Watch how a Gen Xer does it. Managers are people too, prone to moods and bad days just like you, and they're not always on their A-game. Which leads us to our final point — don't take things personally.

Don't Take Things Personally

Every generation struggles with taking things too personal! But know this; just because someone does not like the way you do something doesn't mean they don't like you. Your position at work is certainly a piece of how you define your purpose and sense of self, but it is not who you are. It's interesting to note that we hear a common refrain from the Millennials we interview, "My job does not define me." But we've seen both sides of the survey. Let's just say that employing that mindset is definitely easier said than done.

SO, BASICALLY...

"Your mistakes will often be more valuable than your successes." Some of the greatest inventions — and recipes! — started as mistakes! What's the secret to turning mistakes into triumphs? Feedback. Unfortunately, Millennials report the absence of helpful feedback as a pretty big frustration in the workplace. The best way to overcome this frustration is to instigate feedback! If your manager doesn't come to you, go to them.

Studies have shown that when people ask for feedback, they feel less uncertainty and ambiguity about their performance and responsibilities at work. Sounds like a nice return-on-investment, right? Studies also show that people who seek feedback are generally happier at work and stay with their employers longer.

Of course there are reasons why people hesitate to ask for feedback, such as the fear of negative feedback or being met with disinterest, but the following advice can help you when seeking feedback at work:

- Manage the concerns that prevent you from seeking feedback. Don't hold yourself back by worrying what people will think if you ask!
- First build a quality relationship, then ask for help (Remember the first skill of building a relationship? This is where your effort will come in handy.)
- Choose the right medium for feedback by matching communication style
- Don't try to read your manager's mind, and be sensitive to their mood by waiting for the right time to get feedback
- Stick to the task at hand by limiting feedback to relevant matters

Lastly, the best advice we can give when it comes to receiving feedback? Don't take things too personally.

GO FOR FEEDBACK

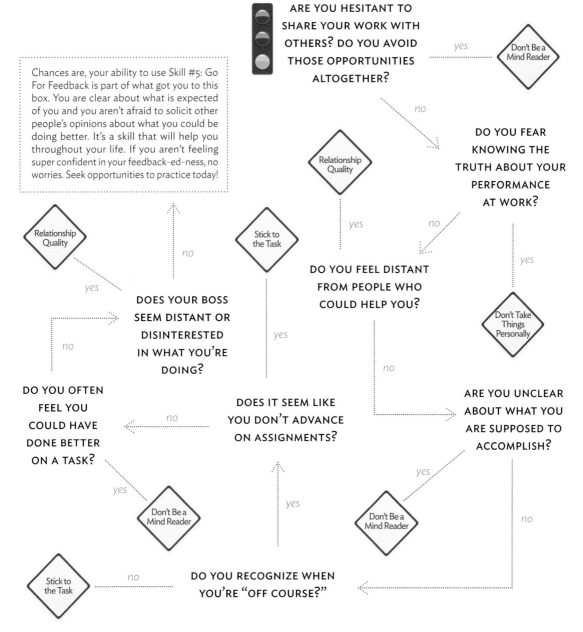

ARE YOU HESITANT TO SHARE YOUR WORK WITH OTHERS? DO YOU AVOID THOSE OPPORTUNITIES ALTOGETHER?

yes → Don't Be a Mind Reader

no

Chances are, your ability to use Skill #5: Go For Feedback is part of what got you to this box. You are clear about what is expected of you and you aren't afraid to solicit other people's opinions about what you could be doing better. It's a skill that will help you throughout your life. If you aren't feeling super confident in your feedback-ed-ness, no worries. Seek opportunities to practice today!

DO YOU FEAR KNOWING THE TRUTH ABOUT YOUR PERFORMANCE AT WORK?

Relationship Quality

yes ... *no*

Relationship Quality

Stick to the Task

yes

DO YOU FEEL DISTANT FROM PEOPLE WHO COULD HELP YOU?

yes

Don't Take Things Personally

DOES YOUR BOSS SEEM DISTANT OR DISINTERESTED IN WHAT YOU'RE DOING?

no

no

yes

DO YOU OFTEN FEEL YOU COULD HAVE DONE BETTER ON A TASK?

no

DOES IT SEEM LIKE YOU DON'T ADVANCE ON ASSIGNMENTS?

no

ARE YOU UNCLEAR ABOUT WHAT YOU ARE SUPPOSED TO ACCOMPLISH?

yes

yes

yes

Don't Be a Mind Reader

Don't Be a Mind Reader

no

Stick to the Task

no

DO YOU RECOGNIZE WHEN YOU'RE "OFF COURSE?"

YOU WON'T BE REWARDED
FOR TRYING HARD;

YOU'LL BE REWARDED
FOR RESULTS.

Chapter 9

BE ACCOUNTABLE

Parents and friends may have let you off the hook a time or two, but chances are your peers, managers, and customers won't care about your excuses for why something didn't happen that was supposed to — or why something did happen that wasn't supposed to! When you agree to be held accountable for specific results, your accomplishments will give you more satisfaction than pulling a quick one on your boss, even if the dog really did eat your report or your tire really was flat. You should know that when it comes to work, you can forget about effort. It's all about the outcome. When you're accountable for the outcome, your accomplishments can create better opportunities for more freedom and responsibility at work.

"Once you've secured new assignments, start asking millions of questions to everyone! No one minds if someone asks a question with a smile, but everyone hates a job done poorly. Figure it out! Make a difference, make your mark! I have always gone into every situation knowing that I will only be given things when I put myself out there and take them. If one way doesn't work, then try and try again until it does work. If there's nothing left to learn in your position, don't complain. Just thank your employer and move on to the next amazing thing." — Ryan

ROADBLOCKS

 "I know two things for sure about them. [Millennials] think everything is negotiable and they never run out of excuses."

Roadblock Challenges	What Millennials Want
Rigid processes	*To have a say in how they do their job*

Rigid processes ahead! One of the first run-ins you will have with management will probably be about how things are done. It won't matter if you find an easier or more proficient way of doing your job. You can argue until you are blue in the face but your ideas or opinions will be readily dismissed until you master their way of doing things.

When surveyed, we heard from managers that Millennials frequently ask to change their schedules, that they tend to question or altogether ignore deadlines, and rather than accepting responsibility for a project that went badly they place blame on the team or department. Whatever the reason is for the behavior managers tell us about, the bottom line is this: there is a perception that Millennials are disengaged, disinterested, and don't care about their work. Does this perception make you angry? It's important to understand that behind every perception there's a reason for it. If enough managers tell us what they see and interpret, and over time our research shows those same trends, at some point we have to step back and look at the data and facts.

Unlike the working generations before you, your work doesn't define you. A balance between your work and personal life is imperative to happiness in your career. You like to have control over when and how you work, and it's become easier and easier to guard your time with more conveniences available than ever before. You can take college courses online, you can have several multi-media conversations at one time while doing the laundry and microwaving lunch, and you don't necessarily have to commute to an office anymore. So what comes across to your manager as being disinterested is you protecting your time by looking for ways to combine the tasks that maybe aren't as important to you so that you can spend more time on the tasks that are. Even better, if you can find a way to combine the elements of work and life that do matter to you, you're in career heaven! Millennials value a blending of work and life. You care about your job and you care about your responsibilities. But the fact remains, Millennials are fiercely protective of their time and have come to expect total flexibility in their schedules. A study of more than 40,000 global participants conducted by PwC, the University of Southern California, and the London Business School looked at the Millennial trend of workplace flexibility and reported the following among key findings:

"While meeting [professional] demands can have significant rewards in an employee's future career (e.g. rapid advancement), Millennials value work/life balance, and the majority of them are unwilling to commit to making work lives an exclusive priority, even with the promise of substantial compensation later on. Millennials want more flexibility, e.g. the opportunity to shift hours to night, if necessary. A significant number want a flexible

To be accountable at work is to show that you can be counted on, that you take ownership of the results you are responsible for, and that your focus is not on the efforts you make but on the outcome you produce.

work schedule so much that they   would be willing to give up pay and delay promotions in order to get it."

When some people think about accountability, they think of it in terms of punishment or reward. This kind of accountability is external accountability, meaning it isn't really connected on the inside, and centers only on the outward consequence of actions. But accountability means more than an annual review, being sent to workplace time-out or your nomination for Employee of the Month. The element of being accountable we want to emphasize is internal accountability. This kind of accountability centers on your personal decision to accept it or not. In fact, you could say that accountability is a state of mind.

In this context, accountability really means to have control over an outcome and to be worthy of being trusted. When you are accountable, you understand that certain outcomes will lie within your control, so you actively monitor the results you are getting. It doesn't mean that you shouldn't ask for help or that things will never happen that are beyond your control. It does mean that you will be the one who knows best how things are going. When you're accountable, you'll have the inside scoop and be able to report on it to other people. You will also see your stock as a valuable employee go up in the eyes of others.

Work place accountability isn't like turning in a high school English paper on time, and it's more complex than when your parents had to remind you (over, and over, and over) to please take out the garbage. To be accountable at work is to show that you can be counted on, that you take ownership of the results you are responsible for, and that your focus is not on the efforts you make but on the outcome you produce. It also includes identifying the people who will be affected by your work, agreeing on how you will measure your progress and success, and

Are Millennials really disinterested? Is it that you really don't care about your work? We don't think so, but there must be a reason why so many of your bosses are expressing the same frustrations!

avoiding making excuses or placing blame if something goes awry. It has been argued that the greater the internal accountability, the less need there is for external accountability. In other words, being trusted for outcomes rather than adhering to what may be a potentially irrelevant procedure. Now on this mission of accountability, should you choose to accept it, what will you be up against? It's important to understand that accountability also hinges on your manager's understanding of organizational reality, because most managers operate on their perceptions of reality, rather than on reality itself.

PERCEIVED WEAKNESS

One perception of your generation is that you are disengaged from your work. Millennials value a balance of work and play and like to have control over how they use their time. We'll take it a step further by saying that balance isn't the only thing you seek. Your generation is great at balancing all kinds of things; what you really want is to blend your work and play. Look at the successful organizations who have figured this out! Some businesses have created a more colorful, playful or active environment for their younger employees, including game tables, bean bags in place of chairs or free space for simply "chillaxing." Millennials like to play at work, and they love to work at play. Unfortunately, most offices aren't like Yahoo, Facebook, or Google, and when you arrive to work you're almost forced to set your need for play aside. This can lead to conflicts in the workplace if a manager perceives that you'd rather be somewhere else or if you use your time at work doing (or playing!) something else.

Are Millennials really disinterested? Is it that you really don't care about your work? We don't think so, but there must be a reason why so many of your bosses are expressing the same frustrations! Read on, and we'll explain what you can do to stand out from the crowd.

The more consistent the behavior, the more we can trust how someone will act in given situations. And as you may have learned from some of your friends, it works in both a negative and positive sense. That being said, think about what you hope others will say about you.

KEYS TO USING THE SKILL

As with any success, there are tips and keys to help you get there. Learning to be accountable is no different, and these following tips are our suggestions for how you can separate yourself from the Millennial throng and stand out as a remarkable employee. But know this; the result of choosing to be accountable will influence how your organization and its leaders perceive you. No matter who has gone before you or what other employees have done, your personal reputation can go a loooooooooooooo — (insert breath here) — ooooooooooong way in reducing any uncertainty others may have regarding your future behavior. The better your reputation, the less you will experience the frustration of having someone looking over your shoulder, watching your every move. And, the more trusted you will be and feel. How's that for a bright ray of sunshine? We'll first address what you can do about internal accountability and then talk about managing external accountability.

INTERNAL ACCOUNTABILITY

To Know You Is To Love You, So Think About What You Want Be Known For

We've all had friends that were known for being flakes. Sure, they say they're in for the road trip and concert. They ask you to buy their ticket and to make all the arrangements, then lo-and-behold-but-not-unexpectedly, they cancel at the last minute and leave you hanging with an extra ticket and a car packed for two. And what about the cheapskates? They always seem to accidentally leave their money at home. Or they order the most expensive dish on the menu (not to mention a few spirits) and want to split the bill evenly when it comes time to pay! Then there's the friend who's always late. Everybody knows to give them a fake time (usually 30 to 45 minutes early, right?) to show up for important events. Using these super scientific methods of observation, we see that reputation is the result of personally observing patterns in behavior and sharing these observations with others. The more consistent the behavior, the more we can trust how someone will act in given situations. And as you may have learned from some of your friends, it works in both a negative and positive sense. That being said, think about what you hope others will say about you.

Be known for being competent. Competence is gained through the practice of continual learning. In his book, *Learning As a Way of Being,* Peter Vaill defines learning as, "... changes a person makes in himself or herself that increase the know-why and/or the know-what and/or the know-how the person possesses with respect to a given subject."[33] It is one thing to pursue formal education or have a lifetime of experience, but it is quite another to change as a result of it. Competence leads to confidence, and when you are confident you naturally deploy your best self.

Be known for being dependable. Actor and director Woody Allen is credited with saying that 80 percent of success is just showing up. Want to know what two of the most common complaints against Millennials are? One, they show up late for work, and two, they are not loyal to the organization. Perhaps these are over-generalized perceptions, but you have the power to change these perceptions by showing up on time with a willingness to learn.

Be known for taking responsibility. Avoid blaming others and making excuses. Have you ever heard of Murphy's Law? It's

I want to be known for:

the idea that if something can go wrong, it most likely will. Unfortunately, work is no exception. When things go wrong, and they sometimes do, avoid pointing the finger at someone else or making excuses to justify your actions. Most managers will understand that honest mistakes do happen, and any seasoned leader will know that some things are simply beyond your control. But imagine how it could set you apart if you were to stand up and take responsibility for your share. Even if something was your fault, just taking ownership of it raises you to a higher level than trying to excuse or blame your way out of it.

Be known for carrying your own weight. We Googled the following: "What does it mean to carry your own weight? "And here is the Wiki answer, "My teenage daughter, who expects everything to be given to her and takes for granted the hard work that it takes to provide for her, is an example of someone who does not and probably will not learn how to carry her own weight."[34] Wow. You can't catch a break anywhere! Even Wiki is whacking you! It's a Wiki-whack, paddle-whack, give Millennials a bone! (Sorry, couldn't resist.) We would like to use the metaphor of "carrying your own weight" as simply doing your part, perhaps even going the extra mile when needed. Be prepared to hear what the people in your office or job site will say about how much weight you should be carrying. That's because it is both an organizational and sociological function. With the exception of pumping free weights at the gym, rarely will you get to set your own weight limit.

If you don't know who Darth Vader is, we suggest you put this book down right now and go check out the Star Wars movies. Seriously. Right. Now.

Be known for your integrity. Warren Bennis, author and widely regarded pioneer of leadership studies, suggests that integrity is made up of three things: ambition, competence, and moral compass.[35] Ambition is a good thing and every human being has a certain degree of it (even that roommate who can't put down the video game controller long enough to take a shower). Competency is being good at something (even video games). And moral compass is having the sense of right or wrong. Taking a shower? Right. Days on end of gaming? Wrong. Bennis uses the image of a three-legged stool to illustrate the point. If you have more of one component of integrity than the other two, the stool becomes unstable. So if you have greater ambition than competence or moral compass, you become like a dictator. Just ask Darth Vader; this is the dark side of ambition. If your competence is greater than your ambition or moral compass, then you are like a hapless technician. Bennis emphasizes that having ambition, competence, and moral compass out of balance creates an "uneasiness" in you, and could cause others to distrust you.

EXTERNAL ACCOUNTABILITY

Now for some keys to help you manage external accountability. Let us be the first to tell you that organizations struggle with holding people accountable. And by this we mean on both ends of the spectrum; from having no accountability at all to a totally dysfunctional, command-and-control environment. Unfortunately, this kind of accountability usually only becomes an issue when something goes wrong. As an example, employee time clocks emerged during the industrial revolution because factory owners were over-working children. Time clocks were a way for factory owners to protect themselves from the scrutiny of labor laws. Today, the time clock is more sophisticated and is used more to protect the interests of the company rather than assuring their compliance with labor laws. The point is that most external accountability is designed for the exceptions, so don't take it personally. Try these tips for managing those external issues should they pop up:

🔑 Ask for the details

If this sounds familiar, that's a good sign! It means you've been paying attention with only the occasional text or FB update distracting you. In Chapter 4 we talked about the skill of asking for details. Well, it applies here too. The first step in being accountable is to simply understand what's expected; both from you and from the project or assignment you're in charge of. There's no better way to determine this than to ask questions! Ask, ask, ask. Impress others with your super-duper skill of asking! Be the company's most prominent pain-in-the-ask! It's important to know what level of control you'll have in any given situation, and what (or who) will be depending on the outcome. And the only way you'll know is to ask.

🔑 Agree on the score

Once you've established who else will be involved in what you're doing, such as a team or your boss, it's helpful to clearly define with each other what both good and bad performance will look like, as well as how you are going to measure the success of your responsibilities. For help with this part, try the following exercise on your own or with others: Think of a task or project you are currently in charge of. Then, write down the top five most important results you are accountable for and how you will measure success (or lack thereof) for each result. You could do this in a notebook or smart phone, but be sure it's in a place where you can refer to it often.

🔑 Stay ahead of the game

By staying focused more on results and less on effort, you can get out in front of most issues. Here are some tips to keep things from going in the wrong direction before it's too late to turn them back around:

Check in early and often. Frequently take a look at the results you're getting and measure them against the outcome you're working toward. Communicate often with your manager about the progress you're making and keep other people informed as necessary.

Ask for help. Unlike cheese, wine, and Miley Cyrus, bad news doesn't usually improve with time. When things get off track, report the news to your manager or someone who can help. The sooner the warning flag is raised, the sooner you can correct what needs to be corrected. It's okay to ask for help, and the skill of knowing when and how to do it will set you apart from the crowd and earn you the trust of those in charge.

Be objective. This can be a hard lesson to learn, but we promise that it will be worth it when you do. You'll need to separate your own performance from any outside factors that are beyond your control. Ask Atlas, it's overwhelming to take on the weight of the world! So pay attention to what you do have control over and what you do not. Communicate these things to your manager so that they are also aware of what lies in your hands.

SO, BASICALLY...

"You won't be rewarded for trying hard; you'll be rewarded for results." There is a perception from older managers that Millennials at work are disengaged and disinterested. Whether it's true or not, you will most likely run into this roadblock in your work experience. It won't be enough just to "try hard" if you want to be noticed. You'll have to create results.

Due to advances in technology and an unprecedented number of conveniences available to you, yours is the first generation that demands a more favorable work/life balance. While you like to guard your time, managers sometimes see this as apathy or lack of engagement when it comes to getting work done. The skill of being accountable will help you to overcome this roadblock and allow you to earn the trust of your managers.

To master the skill of accountability, implement the following tips:
- Decide what characteristics you want to be known for — your reputation will often precede you
- Develop dependability, responsibility, and carry your own weight
- Ask for details (this should sound familiar by now!)
- Between you and your manager, agree on how "the score" will be kept
- Stay ahead of the game by checking in early and often, asking for help, and staying objective

Though it's important to be accountable, it doesn't mean you have to responsible for every single thing in your workplace. After all, you're not Atlas and the world doesn't belong on your shoulders. Be clear about what you have control over and what you do not, then be accountable for what does lie in your hands.

BE ACCOUNTABLE

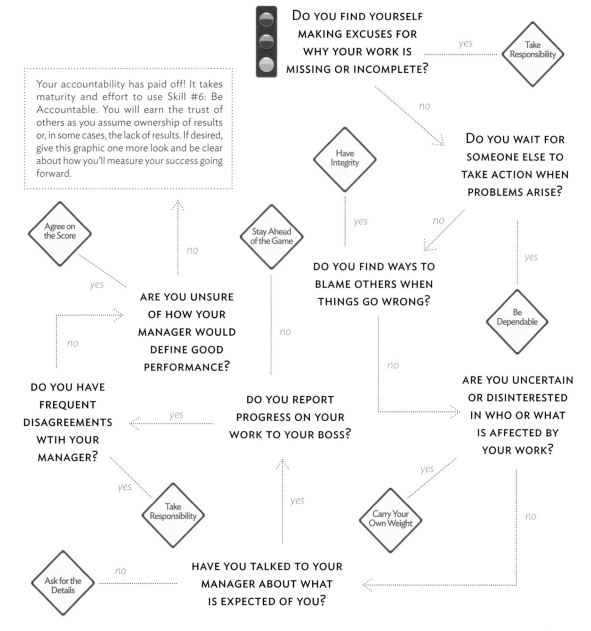

DO YOU FIND YOURSELF MAKING EXCUSES FOR WHY YOUR WORK IS MISSING OR INCOMPLETE?

yes ········· Take Responsibility

no

Your accountability has paid off! It takes maturity and effort to use Skill #6: Be Accountable. You will earn the trust of others as you assume ownership of results or, in some cases, the lack of results. If desired, give this graphic one more look and be clear about how you'll measure your success going forward.

DO YOU WAIT FOR SOMEONE ELSE TO TAKE ACTION WHEN PROBLEMS ARISE?

Have Integrity

Agree on the Score

yes

no

Stay Ahead of the Game

yes

no

DO YOU FIND WAYS TO BLAME OTHERS WHEN THINGS GO WRONG?

ARE YOU UNSURE OF HOW YOUR MANAGER WOULD DEFINE GOOD PERFORMANCE?

no

yes

Be Dependable

no

no

DO YOU HAVE FREQUENT DISAGREEMENTS WTIH YOUR MANAGER?

yes ········· **DO YOU REPORT PROGRESS ON YOUR WORK TO YOUR BOSS?**

ARE YOU UNCERTAIN OR DISINTERESTED IN WHO OR WHAT IS AFFECTED BY YOUR WORK?

no

yes

yes

Take Responsibility

yes

Carry Your Own Weight

yes

no

Ask for the Details

no ········· **HAVE YOU TALKED TO YOUR MANAGER ABOUT WHAT IS EXPECTED OF YOU?**

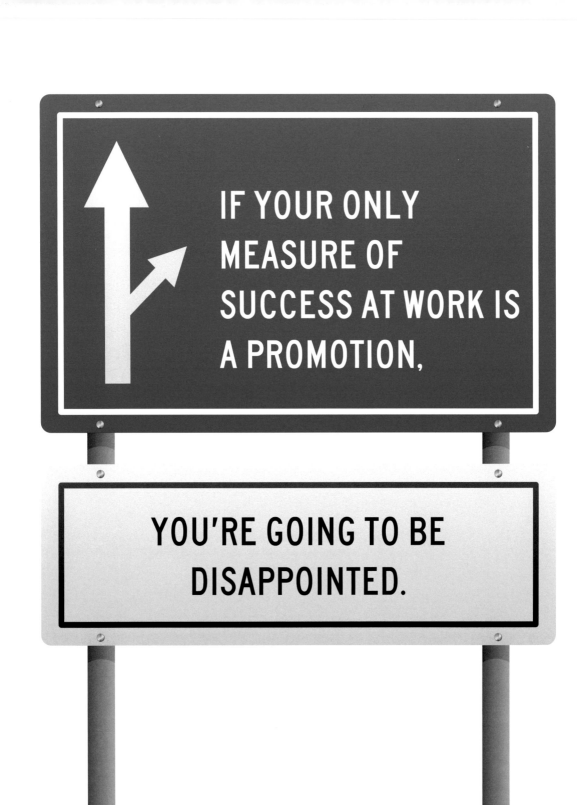

Chapter 10

RECOGNIZE YOUR VALUE

Up until you entered the workforce, your world prepared you to expect success and was set up by everyone around you to practically guarantee it! Once you actually start working, however (we hate to say it, but …) all bets are off. There are no guarantees that you'll be president of the company by Friday. But there is something you can do; align your abilities and expectations with those of your organization in order to make the right contributions for the right rewards. When you know what you are worth, you'll stay on the same page with your managers and be prepared to make a difference.

ROADBLOCK

 "It drives me nuts how they come in and immediately start criticizing what we have been doing."

Roadblock Challenges	What Millennials Want
To be rewarded for work	*Being perceived as entitled*

Many Millennial employees enter the workplace with the belief that they can re-invent the wheel, and they're eager to get started on that wheel within the first week at a new job. Often, Millennials dismiss the way things are done, thinking of methods and processes as "outdated" or "stupid," and aren't too shy about communicating their opinions to older coworkers. Here's a less-than-top-secret tip that may help, should you find yourself in this position: Unless you've been specifically hired to do so, most companies aren't looking to be reinvented — even if you're completely capable of doing it.

*You want your organization to see you as someone with great potential,
someone worth investing in, but proving your value can be tricky.*

All of the other roadblocks your generation experiences at work contribute to this one final challenge: "If I can't use my super-human Millennial strengths, how am I supposed to prove my value?" After all, doing so will be the gateway to your ultimate success. You want your organization to see you as someone with great potential, someone worth investing in, but proving your value can be tricky. The challenge is that many of the good ideas, even great ideas, produced by Millennials don't take into consideration the hard-won experience and reasoning behind the way (and "why") things are done in the workplace. And in some cases, even when the idea or innovation has been brilliant, the way the Millennial employee presents it comes across as so arrogant that managers become less receptive or even worse, totally unwilling to listen to the pitch.

Proving personal value is a challenge for workers of all generations. One of the reasons why it's difficult is that we don't always know where we will add the best value to our organizations. It's like a special teams player in football. You may think you are a great skill player (running back, receiver, tight end) but your greatest contribution to the team may be in covering kick-offs. There have been many National Football League players who eventually enjoyed incredible careers, but started out as special teams standouts.[36] The point is that our competencies have to intersect with what our organizations need.

PERCEIVED WEAKNESS

Believe us when we say that we've done our share of research on generational differences at work. Really. Done. Some research. Probably more than our fair share. (But really, isn't there plenty of research to go around?) We've conducted surveys, collected data, questioned, poked and prodded, observed and studied, and met with leaders and managers across a variety of

Any guess what's the most common complaint we've heard about your peers? If you guessed 'mismanaged expectations', you're right.

organizations and industries. And while it's all been incredibly interesting, we've definitely seen some common threads and themes emerge when your bosses tell us about their experiences working with Millennials. Any guess what's the most common complaint we've heard about your peers? If you guessed 'mismanaged expectations', you're right.

Managers tell us that Millennials seem to expect certain guarantees from work and demonstrate unrealistic expectations about how quickly they should advance. Just as a new business owner can't open up shop expecting their customers to guarantee the business's success, employees can't expect their company to reward them on a no-matter-what basis, or unlike soccer practice, just for "showin' up." According to our studies, young employees often expected — at times even demanded — promotions, raises or bonuses far more quickly than the policies and practices of the organization allowed.

By realistically aligning your expectations with those of your company and understanding how you can best contribute in your role, you'll set yourself up to succeed and take your name right off that Number One complaint list.

MILLENNIAL VALUE

Now, in defense of your generation, this patting-yourself-on-the-back attitude at work isn't completely without reason. You have a lot to be proud about. Seriously! Millennials have extremely well-developed imaginations and problem solving abilities, with the technological skill set to

Check out Saturday Night Live's spoof about just how well you can do anything. Even when anything is pretty much nothing.

back it up and confidence to see it through. The conflict managers and Millennials face resides in what you do with these abilities.

Chances are, behind the need to showcase your mad brain skillz, there's an underlying desire to be recognized. There's a reason for this desire, just as there's a reason for each of the perceptions and values we've discussed so far. We've talked about how your generation was raised with a "You can do anything!" emphasis, along with a "Trophies for everyone!" system of reward. You thrive on recognition! You've grown up looking for it and finding it with less effort than previous generations. So if recognition is something you crave, try this crazy approach at work: Do it their way first. Do it effectively. Then, once you've shown your ability to work with established processes and methods, offer your ideas for improvement. Instead of receiving negative recognition for asking for more responsibility than you've earned, you'll receive positive recognition for learning the ropes and finding ways to improve.

KEYS TO USING THE SKILL

Are you destined to spend your days pondering the demise of so many great ideas (if only they would listen!)? Will you grow old watching that workplace wheel groan painstakingly along, while you sharpen pencils and dream of the wheel you could have built? Only if that's what you want. But if it isn't, here are some keys to recognizing your value so that you can contribute in a meaningful way.

Rather than thinking about the title or job you think you deserve right off the bat, focus on making a difference where you are right now. Not only will you feel happier and more fulfilled at work — regardless of your current position — you'll also show your managers that you are capable of handling more responsibility.

⚷ Know where you fit

Understand what's expected of you in your position at work. (Don't forget the advice to ask for the details!) Think about your values, skills, and abilities (why not make a list?), and look for ways they could line up with those expectations. Then, see how you could make the biggest difference possible in your current position. Rather than thinking about the title or job you think you deserve right off the bat, focus on making a difference where you are right now. Not only will you feel happier and more fulfilled at work — regardless of your current position — you'll also show your managers that you are capable of handling more responsibility. Recognizing your value will help you earn the right kind of attention when it comes time for managers to discuss employees and promotions.

⚷ Align your expectations

Avoid making unrealistic assumptions about rewards, raises or promotions at work. To align your own personal expectations with the reality of where you work and what you do, see if you can find answers to the following questions:

1. What specific things have people achieved to receive promotions at work? How long did it take for them to be promoted?
2. What happens if someone submits an idea that is implemented at work? Are they rewarded, and if so, how?
3. What rewards, if any, have people received in the past? For example, when they worked extra hours, put in long days or went the extra mile on a project?
4. What kinds of skills and accomplishments do leaders in the company have?

🔑 *Learn how to handle the mismatches*

Like the yoga pants you ordered online last month, not every investment is a perfect fit. Your expectations and experiences at work are no exception. Sometimes, you'll find that what you want and what your manager wants are two very different things. If this situation sounds familiar, try asking yourself the following questions. And don't forget to go for feedback as needed.

- Is this something I can influence? Am I able to change my expectations?
- Am I able to change the environment around me so that it fits within my expectations?
- Am I in the right place? Is this the right position, organization, career, etc. for me? If not, where and how could I find a better match?
- Do I have the right skills and experience for the situation or position? Is this an opportunity for me to grow and develop, or not?

🔑 *Play to your strengths*

Did you honestly think we would write a book about Millennials and not take the page space to tell you how great you are? The truth is, when you consider what your generation is prepared to offer to businesses, communities, and organizations around the globe, you have a lot going for you and a lot to give. Your skill set is unique and relevant to the way work happens today. We asked Millennial study participants this question: "As a young worker, what

The truth is, when you consider what your generation is prepared to offer to businesses, communities, and organizations around the globe, you have a lot going for you and a lot to give. Your skill set is unique and relevant to the way work happens today.

While conducting research, Millennials were asked what they saw as their number one challenge in the workplace. The majority of respondents gave one of the two following answers: a lack of experience or not being taken seriously.

advantage do you think you have in the workplace?" Specific themes bubbled to the surface almost immediately and were very clear.

Millennial Advantages
• Technologically savvy
• Fresh education/perspective
• Energy
• Social networking ability
• Flexibility
• Global mindset
• Creativity
• Teachable
• Tolerant
• Goal oriented

What would you add to this list? Interestingly, managers agree with Millennials about the advantages they perceive to have in the workplace. Managers in our study preferred having Millennials on their team over other generations when it came to change initiatives or trying something new. They love your energy and that you are so creative. Embracing diversity is something that comes rather naturally to your generation. This is a gigantic plus when it comes to workplace morale and productivity.

We asked Millennials to give us specific examples of how they've been able to apply these advantages at work, either to get ahead or to create needed solutions to a workplace problem. Here's what they had to say:

Technologically Savvy: "I've had older managers that weren't in tune with technology. Although my way of doing things might have not always been the most traditional, they often created efficiencies for the company in the long term. To overcome my manager's hesitation to technology, I got him engaged in the process early on to get his buy-in on approaching a situation differently. Once I got his blessing, I used a more updated technical method and was able to show him the before and after picture." — Dustin

Fresh Education / Perspective: "After graduation, I made the decision within the company I worked for to pursue a totally different career track. To do so, I had to step down two levels to be hired in a new department. Though it was immediately evident that I was leaps and bounds ahead of others on my team, I tried to focus on doing my job well and setting aside my own predetermined levels of effort or performance that I thought would be required to advance. At times it was really hard to see others be promoted around me, but I had to learn patience. I had to rely on the assurance that my education was relevant and trust that a moment of sacrifice would be worth it in the end. I learned to be vocal about what I wanted and about where I wanted to go. But overall, being patient ended up being my greatest strength." — Lauren

Energetic: "I am self-employed, I run a non-profit with my best friends. We have trust, loyalty, and respect for each other which helps us to work in a high-energy and fast-paced environment. I love team work and collaborating to share and develop new ideas. What I love the most is that we don't feel the need to always be right, just to have made the right decision at the end of every meeting. We thrive on the energy we get and give to each other." — Ray

Socially Connected / Networking Ability: "One of my previous employers didn't understand how to use Twitter or any other social media outlets. When I was hired, I took over that part of the company. The business had only nine followers on Twitter when I took over the account. After three months, I had increased their followers by 700%. Where my employer saw Twitter as simply a tool for advertising, I used it as a way to get our company socializing with the community. I worked very hard to increase those numbers and felt great about what I was able to do for the company's social media side." — Bethany

Flexible: "I began my job with literally no tasks, no tools, and no goals or guidance outside of my job description. So, I decided just to work like crazy! I went outside of my cubicle and grabbed people to help me figure things out and find the information I needed. They love me here, and just a few months ago I was promoted into a sales position! I'm three months into the new year and even though I still don't know my sales quota for the year, I am just working as hard as I can and being flexible." — Paul

Globally Minded: "I worked for a huge international software company that was quickly expanding into foreign markets. They started out with kind of a one-pitch-fits-all sales approach, without really considering the culture and customs of the new markets and clients. I was sent to help open an area in a different country, and it quickly became evident that a standard way of marketing wasn't working. Along with a team of salespeople, I set out to better understand the way business was done in this part of the world, and went back to the company with suggestions for how we could better meet the needs of our international customers. We came up with a more customized approach and the results were incredible. Now, as a company, we're more mindful of how business is done outside of the United States." — Peter

Creative: "I was put in charge of a particular function within our department. I was given full support and free rein to develop a process for the function. I first looked at how it had been done in the past, then looked at what went well and what pieces were missing. I talked with other individuals who we served through this function and developed a new process which closed some gaps and made for a better experience for our customers." — Jessie

Teachable: "There have been numerous times when me and my boss have been on different pages because we focus on different aspects of the department and organization, but I appreciate her view and can see where she's coming from. It has actually really helped me grow and make better decisions within my position. I like to hear what is important to my boss because it helps me see what direction to take or how to better argue my position in an issue if I disagree." — Joy

Tolerant: "In the back of my mind, I have had to tell myself, 'I may not really care, but I always have to try my hardest and treat this like it's my own idea coming to life.' This approach to tasks I don't care about has helped me put more effort into things I had no passion for." — Theresa

Goal Oriented: "The company I worked for wasn't utilizing technology as well as they could have, and the day-to-day tasks were becoming really inefficient and ineffective. I worked nights and weekends to find answers to the company's problems. Six months later I presented some solutions to the Director of Operations. A year later, nothing had been done, so I went directly to the CEO and presented the problems I had observed as well as the solutions I had come up with. It turned out very good for me, but not so good for the Director of Operations. The CEO confronted him about not considering my ideas. The director was unwilling to try new things and refused to learn the new technology that would make our work flow more productive. He was let go, and two years later, I was promoted into his position." — Ross

SO, BASICALLY...

"If your only measure of success at work is a promotion, you're going to be disappointed." We don't mean to be a Debbie-Downer, but it's true. In today's workplace, the measure of success has a wide library of definitions. Managers perceive Millennials as being entitled, when what you want is to be rewarded and recognized for your efforts.

To overcome this roadblock you'll need to realistically align your expectations with those of your company and understand how you can best contribute and make a difference.

To develop the skill of recognizing your value, seek to:
- Know where you fit within your organization, then make the best difference you can make
- Align your own expectations for advancement by asking questions such as, "What specific things have people achieved to receive promotions? How long did it take for them to be promoted? What kinds of accomplishments have leaders within the company made and what skills do they have?"
- Learn how to handle the mismatches when they happen ... because they will
- Play to your strengths

Speaking of strengths in the workplace, Millennials are brimming with them. Your generation is know for its strengths which translate into workplace advantages. Among those advantages are technologically savvy, fresh perspective and advanced education, social networking abilities, flexibility, global mindedness, creativity and teachability, tolerance and extreme goal setting.

RECOGNIZE YOUR VALUE

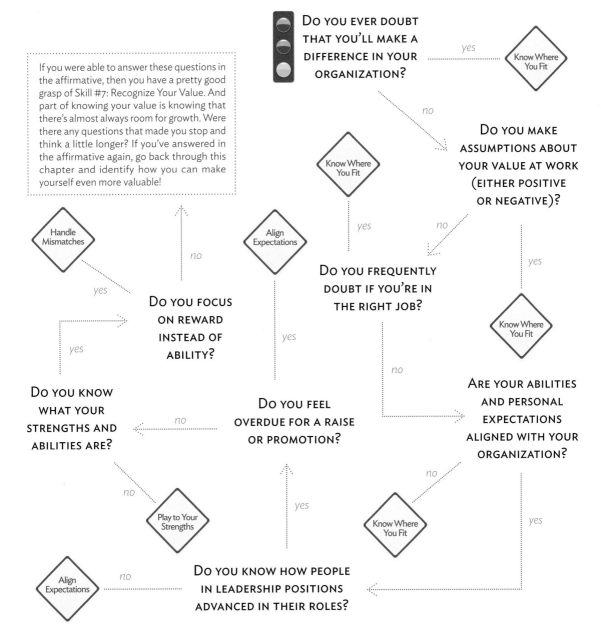

If you were able to answer these questions in the affirmative, then you have a pretty good grasp of Skill #7: Recognize Your Value. And part of knowing your value is knowing that there's almost always room for growth. Were there any questions that made you stop and think a little longer? If you've answered in the affirmative again, go back through this chapter and identify how you can make yourself even more valuable!

Do you ever doubt that you'll make a difference in your organization?

yes → Know Where You Fit

no → **Do you make assumptions about your value at work (either positive or negative)?**

Know Where You Fit

yes ↓ **Do you frequently doubt if you're in the right job?**

no → Know Where You Fit *yes*

Align Expectations

yes ↓ **Do you feel overdue for a raise or promotion?**

Handle Mismatches

yes → **Do you focus on reward instead of ability?**

no ↑

yes → **Do you know what your strengths and abilities are?** ← *no*

no → Play to Your Strengths

yes ↑

Align Expectations — *no* → **Do you know how people in leadership positions advanced in their roles?**

no → **Are your abilities and personal expectations aligned with your organization?**

no → Know Where You Fit *yes*

← **Do you know how people in leadership positions advanced in their roles?**

FIRST LEARN THE GROUND RULES. THEN YOU CAN DECIDE TO BREAK THEM.

Chapter 11

THE TOP FIVE MISTAKES MILLENNIALS MAKE @ WORK

(And how to avoid being THAT Millennial who makes them.)

Like body builders and baby oil, you're all slathered up and ready to go. Slathered in skillzzz, that is. You have what it takes to be greater than you were just a hundred pages ago. Sure, we've given plenty of warnings and loads of things to look out for, but we're not quite done with the warnings yet. Maybe it's our older-generational-tendency-of-always-telling-you-what-you-should-be-doing-differently, but we couldn't *not* mention this next part.

Just like every other generation, sometimes Millennials make mistakes. Sometimes, large numbers of Millennials make mistakes. Ironically, sometimes large numbers of Millennials make the exact same mistakes. And as a Millennial, you are at risk of making them. Managers and businesses across the board have told us so, and the proof is in the pudding. When enough companies tell us what they see, we pay attention. We hope that you will, too. The best way to avoid making the same mistakes that hundreds of thousands of Millennials are making, is to

The best way to avoid making the same mistakes that hundreds of thousands of Millennials are making, is to know what those mistakes are.

know what those mistakes are. Check out these workplace mishaps, then get out there and avoid 'em!

Job hopping

An article in *Forbes* magazine calls the Millennial trend of job-hopping the "new normal." For older generations, loyalty to work used to rank right up there with loyalty to country and family. Try asking an older worker to wrap their brain around today's short-lived career stints lasting all of three minutes! According to the Bureau of Labor Statistics in 2012, the average tenure of workers was 4.4 years per job. However, the expected tenure of today's youngest work-force is half that amount — barely over two years. At this rate, you can expect to have almost 20 different jobs over the course of your lifetime! Why is this a bad thing, you ask?

Did you know that job instability could cost you your dream job? Recruiters and human resource workers routinely screen out chronic job hoppers, opting instead for appli-cants with proven longevity. Most recruiters will assume you didn't learn much as it takes anywhere from six months to a year to become fully proficient at a job. And most of the time your resume and abridged job history (oh wait, that was the full version?) will tell your story long before you get a chance to add your two cents! By the way, it is a myth that managers don't care about tenure at work. They do.

When it comes to work, there may be the notion that the grass is always greener on the other side. So here's our advice if you often find yourself staring out the window at the pasture across the street: If you feel unhappy or dissatisfied at every and any job, stop assuming it's the job. You may want to spend less time job-hunting and more time skill-building.

Asking for a raise at the wrong time or in the wrong way

When it comes to making sushi, there's definitely a right way and a wrong way to do it. Done correctly, it can be a wonderfully rewarding experience, dripping in wasabi and soy. Done incorrectly, you'll enjoy a not-so-scenic ride on the Porcelain Express. All. Night. Long. We're not saying that you shouldn't ask for a raise (even though it's unheard of for older workers to pre-empt annual reviews by asking for one) or that you should pass on sushi for dinner. We're suggesting that before you bound into your manager's office with a demand to make what the CEO makes, take a minute to think things through. As with sushi prep, there is a right way to go about it — resulting in a much more pleasant experience.

For starters, if you ask for a raise prematurely or without considering your company's stand on raises and promotions, you are actually contributing to a huge stereotype that managers have of your generation. There is the perception that Millennials have unrealistic expectations about advancement and promotions, and that they are driven by feelings of entitlement. Don't be the reason for the stereotype; be the exception! By knowing the "rules" of raises and recognition, you won't blow the hard-earned reputation you've already won. Just as you wouldn't visit a foreign country without first researching its culture, don't put yourself above your company's culture and established way of doing things. Especially when it comes to money! Research your company's policies and work within the proper frame, keeping in mind that you and your workplace are involved in a value-exchange. You agree to work. They agree to pay you. End of story.

If you do feel a raise is warranted, be sure to build a solid case before you present it to your manager. Base your request on performance rather than need. Don't prepare a PowerPoint highlighting your sorrowful monthly expenses, budget, and financial woes. But do be prepared to wow the hierarchy's socks off with facts concerning your contributions, achievements, performance, and value.

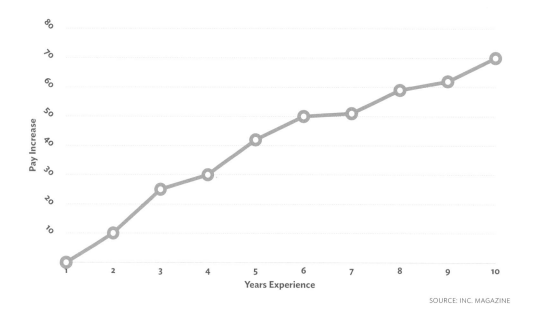

SOURCE: INC. MAGAZINE

Expecting your boss to take care of you

They're not there to hold your hand. Enough said? Don't wait for permission or a hand-embossed invitation to rock it at work. Take the initiative to show your boss that you're there to take care of him. Trust us on this one. YOU will be the rock star, and we can't wait to read the book you'll write in a few years about how you did it.

This approach to catering to an authority figure could be a bit of a shift for Millennial workers, because as we discussed earlier, adults in your childhood and adolescent life seemed to exist primarily to cater to you. With a little fine-tuning, you'll get more comfortable with managing the expectations of your boss that are realistic and learning to discard those expectations that are not. The ideal outcome is a symbiotic give-and-take relationship between you and your leaders, where both parties get what they need and learn to count on each other.

Underestimating older people

Here's an interesting dichotomy — Millennials face steep and sometimes harsh stereotypes. Yet they enter the workforce and, sha-ziiing! Some Millennials likewise apply steep and harsh stereotypes to the older people they work with. It's a no-win, right? As much as your generation feels discounted by others, the Millennial generation is equally prone to discounting those with more years under their belt. And by more years, we don't mean decades upon decades of more years. It's not just the Builders and Boomers that are falling victim to underestimation. Sometimes it's the workers just one generation ahead of yours!

There is value in considering the opinions and experiences of those who've been around the block a few times. They may have seen trends come and go, employees come and go, hairstyles  (or hair!) come and go. All of this knowledge could be of benefit to you in some future day.

What happens if you become too quick to discount older workers? You not only lose the opportunity to meet some really remarkable people (who doesn't love hearing stories that begin with the words "Back in the day"?), you also lose the tacit wisdom, experience, skills, and insight they hold. Usually, when someone is appointed as a leader, there's a reason why. Try to learn about what they know; because it's what they know that led them to where they are.

Expecting work to always be fun

Have you ever been invited to a party that you were really excited about? You carefully laid out your rico-suave party outfit, maybe even scheduled a back-wax, and counted down the days. When the big night arrives, you knock at the door, polished and shined and ready for fun. But to your dismay, you are handed not a red plastic cup, but a bucket of PineSol and some smelly old rags. There is no party. It was a ruse! You were invited there to work. Okay, so this probably hasn't happened. (Maybe that one time at your grandma's house.) But if you were expecting a party and instead received work, you'd be sorely disappointed, right?

So why then, if you're headed to work, would you be disappointed that there's no party going on when you get there? Sorry to say it, but for the majority of hours you'll spend at work, you'll be ... working. Because, well, that's what work is. Work. A common Millennial mistake is the expectation that work should be fun! Yeah, man! But most of the time, work just isn't. Sure, there will be times for socializing and laughing, but unless you're a professional clown it won't be your standard workload to tell jokes and liven the place up.

Our advice on the matter is this: Evaluate how you define fun. Gone are the carefree days of swashbuckling and lolly-gagging (truthfully, we don't even know what these things are). Think about what it is you really want from work. Do you want accomplishment? Recognition? Satisfaction? Income? Stability? Or is it really just fun you seek? If you're unable to reconcile your need for fun with a basic need for income, perhaps you'd enjoy a volunteer position at Disneyland. Or making balloon animals at the zoo? Maybe somewhere there's a daily parade in need of a float-riding-taffy-tosser. But if you can adjust your need for fun and are willing to look at what may bring a greater feeling of satisfaction to your life, expect to spend most of your hours at work — you guessed it — working.

Chapter 12

A FEW FINAL WORDS OF ADVICE

com•mence•ment: a beginning or start

Like ice cream cones, your favorite movie, vacations, and this book, all good things must come to an end. Which for us, is now. But don't despair! Though you've reached the end (unless you plan to read the endnotes — have fun with that!), you're really arriving at the beginning ... of greatness! We know you have already accomplished wonderful and important things, but we also know that as you develop and practice these skills in work and life, you will find yourself growing into a new and improved level of Millennial awesomeness. As you embark on this new commencement, please consider a few last words of advice from our generation's desk to yours.

Be the first to adapt

We have trained thousands of managers on how to better work with you and your Millennial colleagues. We repeatedly tell the managers we train that the people with the most responsibility should be the ones to adapt first. That being said, if you want more opportunity and responsibility at work, beat your manager to the punch by being the first to adapt. In a perfect world where clouds rain glitter and people travel by flying elephant, managers would understand your generational differences. But hopefully by now, you get that most do not. As long as clouds continue to rain plain old rain (unless you live near a toxic waste site — in which case, you get really interesting rain), see what happens when you take the initiative to adapt first.

Adapt for the right reasons

The perceptions managers have of Millennials are real and will create a reality you have to work with. But the last thing we want is for you to think the solution is to simply manipulate how you are perceived by acting or putting on an insincere show. It didn't work for the vertically-challenged Wizard of Oz, and it won't work for you. The two-fold belief of our work is this: that you are misunderstood by older generations who currently make the rules at work, and that the skills in this book will help you overcome not only other people's perceptions but your own challenges as well. Our intent is not for you to simply mimic older employees or be the office brown-noser. We hope that you will seek to understand other generations, connect with them, and be authentic in your desire to adapt.

Get the manager you want

In our experience working with organizations and businesses around the world, we have come across some incredible managers out there, and we hope you get one that seeks to understand you and is committed to your success. But if by chance you don't get an all-star rock'n'roller, don't give up. This book is about helping you see that there is always something you can do to keep moving forward. The greater sense you have of being in control of your future, the easier it will be to take action when you feel down or defeated. Practicing the seven skills will help you get the manager you want and help your manager get the employee they want! So do yourself and your career a favor. Use and apply these skills before you call it quits.

Pay attention to what older generations already know

Think of it as a kind of osmosis; the assimilation of ideas, knowledge, and information by simply being around it. Use the power of osmosis to harness the expertise of those you work with. Sure, you could take the next several decades to learn it all on your own — if you wanted to — or, you could just pay attention to what older workers are trying to teach you and save yourself the next thirty years of learning by trial and error. You know, whichever makes more sense to you. But seriously, there is great value in learning from those who have already learned. Be teachable, be interested, and pay attention. You'll be amazed at what information you can gather just by looking to those who've been at it longer than you have.

And the last word, if you don't like it, learn about it and change it

Let's be honest. All the progress we've made as a species has been done by people who saw an opportunity to make things different or better. You and your peers are going to change the world in (hopefully) fantastic ways. You will change the workplace, too. Your ethics, your creativity, and your hard work will have a huge impact. So, don't take anything we've mentioned in this book as a warning not to try and change things for the better. Our goal is simply to point out the obstacles that you will face along the way, and to avoid the frustration that may come with them. All the skills in this book are tools you can use to move forward, they aren't here to hold you back.

So, that's it. That's our advice. Throw it in with all the other advice from parents, teachers, aunts, uncles, coaches, older siblings, and everyone else who shares their 'secrets' of success with you. But the experience doesn't have to end here. We'd love to hear from you about your challenges, success stories, and your own advice for other Millennials.

Visit us at: www.MillennialsAtWork.com and join the conversation. See you there!

We wish you success, happiness, and a fantastic career.

Endnotes

1 *Pew Research Center: http://www.pewsocialtrends.org/files/2010/10/millennials-confident-connected-open-to-change.pdf*

2 *Pew Research Study: December 2009 Current Population Study (CPS)*

3 *Bureau of Labor Statistics 2011*

4 *Mitchell, A. (2013) The rise of the millennial workforce. Wired Magazine. Retrieved from http://www.wired.com/2013/08/the-rise-of-the-millennial-workforce/*

PwC, PwC's Nextgen: A Global Generational Study (2013). Report on an evolving talent strategy to matc the new workforce reality. Retrieved from http://www.pwc.com/en_US/us/people-management/publications/assets/pwc-nextgen-summary-of-findings.pdf

5 *Bloomberg BusinessWeek, July 2007. "Children of the Web"*

6 *www.drspock.com/about*

7 *http://www.krochetkids.org/who-we-are/our-story/*

8 *http://www.planetofsuccess.com/blog/2011/developing-empathy-walk-a-mile-in-someone's-shoes/*

9 *http://money.usnews.com/money/personal-finance/articles/2013/03/12/what-its-really-like-to-live-on-a-shoestring-budget*

10 *http://usatoday30.usatoday.com/news/education/2010-02-24-millennials24_st_n.htm*

11 *Maslow, A. H. (1943). A Theory of Human Motivation. Psychological Review*

12 *Rath, Tom (2006). Vital friends. New York: Gallup*

13 Grenier, Amanda (2007). "Crossing age and generational boundaries: Exploring intergenerational research encounters". Journal of Social Issues 63 (4): 718.

14 Wheatley, Margaret (2002). Turning to one another: simple conversations to restore hope to the future. San Francisco: Berrett-Koehler.

15 Ury, William (1993). Getting past no:negotiating your way from confrontation to cooperation (rev, ed.). New York: Bantam

16 Smith, Rod (2006, March 25). Differentiation of self. Difficult Relationships, 1(4). Retrieved January 12, 2013, from http://www.difficultrelationships.com/2006/03/25/bowen-differentiation/

17 Covey, Stephen (1989). The Seven Habits of Highly Effective People. New York: Simon & Schuster.

18 Goelman, D. (1996). Emotional intelligence: why it can matter more than IQ. New York: Bantam.

19 Espinoza, et al. (2010). Managing the millennials: discover the core competencies for managing today's workforce. New Jersey: Wiley.

20 Wheatley, M. (2002). Turning to one another: simple conversation to restore hope to the future. San Francisco: Berrett-Koehler. P. 34

21 http://www.searchquotes.com/quotation/ Just_because_everything_is_different_doesn't_mean_anything_has_changed./157139/

22 Senge, P. (1990). The fifth discipline. New York: Currency Doubleday.

23 Popcorn, F. (1991). The popcorn report. New York: Currency Doubleday

24 Erickson, T. J., Alsop, R., Nicholson, P., & Miller, J. (2009). Gen Y in the workforce Harvard Business School Publication Corp.

25 "In Defense of Distraction", Sam Anderson. New York Magazine May 2009.

26 "Is Multitasking Bad For Us?", Brandon Keim, NOVA. http://www.pbs.org/wgbh/nova/body/is-multitasking-bad.html

27 "Internet Addiction: The New Mental Health Disorder?", Alice Walton. Forbes October 2012.

28 Stobbeleir, K., Ashford, S., & Buyens, D. (2011). Self-regulation of creativity at work: The role of feedback-seeking behavior in creative performance. Academy of Management Journal, Volume (54)4. 811-831.

29 Madzar, S. (1995). Feedback seeking behavior: A review of the literature and implications for hrd practitioners. Human Resource Development Quarterly, Volume 6(4). 337-349.

30 Madzar, S. (1995). Feedback seeking behavior: A review of the literature and implications for hrd practitioners. Human Resource Development Quarterly, Volume 6(4). 337-349.

31 VandeWalle, D. (1995). A goal orientation model of feedback seeking behavior. Unpublished. Doctoral dissertation. University of Minnesota, Minneapolis.

32 Ashford, S. (1986). Feedback-seeking in individual adaptation: A resource perspective. Academy of Management Journal, Volume (29)3. 465-487.

33 Vaill, P. (1996). Learning as a way of being. San Francisco: Jossey-Bass (p. 21).

34 http://wiki.answers.com/Q/What_does_it_mean_to_carry_your_own_weight (Retrieved April 11, 2013)

35 http://en.wikipedia.org/wiki/Warren_Bennis

36 http://www.sportingcharts.com/dictionary/nfl/special-teams.aspx

LEARN MORE

Businesses are struggling to keep pace with a new generation of young people entering the workforce who have starkly different attitudes and desires than the employees of the past few decades. Whether you are a Manager, a Millennial or an Employee that works with Millennials and you're trying to answer the question, How can I improve my effectiveness?, here are some next steps...

MILLENNIALS@**WORK**

Growing up, Millennials faced a very different set of rules in their lives than they will in the workplace. Many Millennials find the traditional workplace a frustrating and challenging experience. Promotions and rewards seem few and far between. They encounter disinterested or even hostile managers who view them as entitled and unrealistic.

The fact is, Millennials have perhaps even more going for them than previous generations, but they need to be prepared with workplace skills (skills they were never taught) that will encourage them to put that potential to use.

Workplace Readiness Assessment (WRA)

Take the WRA to discover your readiness in seven key areas that have a significant impact on your success in the workplace and provide you with a score based on the average responses of your peers.

MILLENNIALS@WORK Training

This course will help Millennial employees develop seven critical skills that will help them find purpose in their work and take their organization to the next level.

- Help them understand their place in history and the potential roadblocks they face with older generations at work.

- Help them understand the different generations in the workplace, their values and priorities.

- Teach them the 7 Skills that research identified as critical for Millennials to succeed.

- Help them understand their paradigms of promotions and rewards at work, and find purpose in their current role.

MANAGING **MILLENNIALS**

According to research, the #1 reason people quit their jobs is because of a poor relationship with their boss. This new generation, the Millennials, is no different. In fact, they value the relationship with their boss even more than previous generations. See why the next generation is different, and how to handle the flood of younger employees into the workplace.

. . . .

Generational Rapport Inventory (GRI)

As an older generation manager, taking the GRI assessment will help you see how you stack up against other managers in nine key areas when working with younger employees.

MANAGING MILLENNIALS Training

This course focuses on specific skills that managers at any level can use to improve the effectiveness of their changing work force by:

- Becoming aware of generational differences in the workforce.
- Learning what works and what doesn't work with Millennial employees based on the research.
- Increasing job satisfaction and retention for them and their employees.
- Unleashing the creativity and potential of your twenty-something employees.

ADDITIONAL TRAINING

THE **CHANGE** ELEMENT

Based on decades of work helping organizations, large and small, change successfully. It provides practical tools, like the Change Model™, to help people understand exactly what happens during change, where they are in the process, and what the next steps should be.

LEADERS@**CHANGE**

Implementing your strategy means that your leaders and managers need to understand how to get people to do things differently. This two-day work session focuses on the strategies, ideas, and tools that your leaders need to make it happen.

THE ULTIMATE COMPETITIVE ADVANTAGE

FranklinCovey is a global company specializing in performance improvement. We help organizations achieve results that require a change in human behavior.

Our expertise is in seven areas:

LEADERSHIP

Develops highly effective leaders who engage others to achieve results.

EXECUTION

Enables organizations to execute strategies that require a change in human behavior.

PRODUCTIVITY

Equips people to make high-value choices and execute with excellence in the midst of competing priorities.

TRUST

Builds a high-trust culture of collaboration and engagement, resulting in greater speed and lower costs.

SALES PERFORMANCE

Transforms the buyer-seller relationship by helping clients succeed.

CUSTOMER LOYALTY

Drives faster growth and improves frontline performance with accurate customer- and employee-loyalty data.

EDUCATION

Helps schools transform their performance by unleashing the greatness in every educator and student.

WWW.FRANKLINCOVEY.COM